REMBRANDT, THE JEWS
AND THE BIBLE

1. Rembrandt, Self-Portrait
Painted by the artist while living in the Jewish quarter of Amsterdam.

REMBRANDT,
THE JEWS AND THE BIBLE

by

FRANZ LANDSBERGER

translated from the German by

FELIX N. GERSON

PHILADELPHIA

THE JEWISH PUBLICATION SOCIETY OF AMERICA

5732–1972

Second Edition, 1961
Fourth Impression, 1972

LIBRARY OF CONGRESS CATALOG CARD NUMBER: 61:12367

PRINTED IN THE UNITED STATES OF AMERICA

FOREWORD

IT has often proved a comfort to me, in this era of European Jewish tragedy, to dwell upon the life and work of Rembrandt. Here was a man of Germanic ancestry who did not regard the Jews in the Holland of his day as a "misfortune," but approached them with friendly sentiments, dwelt in their midst, and portrayed their personalities and ways of life. Rembrandt, moreover, regarded the Bible as the greatest Book in the world and held it in reverent affection all his life, in affluence and poverty, in success and failure. He never wearied in his devotion to biblical themes as subjects for his paintings and other graphic presentations, and in these portrayals he was the first to have the courage to use the Jews of his environment as models for the heroes of the sacred narratives.

I have frequently referred to these remarkable facts in lectures delivered in Germany and later in America, and have felt it incumbent upon me to convey to others the solace I experienced in their contemplation. I desired, also, to furnish my coreligionists with an understanding of what Rembrandt had done for them, and to bring to them a recognition of their debt to his art, which was so wide in scope and so rich in spirit.

These considerations influenced me to prepare the following pages, which do not present the whole of Rembrandt, but merely that phase of his life and work which has bearing upon his relation to the Jews and to their Holy Scriptures. This phase, however, should prove the more deeply satisfying to us, because it lay not upon the periphery of his personality, but at its very core. For this reason I offer the present work to the consideration of those who, like myself, aspire to a deeper understanding of the phenomenon that was Rembrandt.

ACKNOWLEDGMENTS

Lady Mary and Professor Gilbert Murray extended to me their gracious hospitality in Oxford, England, during those many months after I had been exiled from Germany and before I could accept the call of the Hebrew Union College in Cincinnati. To their memory I dedicate this volume as a partial expression of my gratitude.

I extend my thanks also to Doctor Wolfgang Stechow of Oberlin College, Oberlin, Ohio, noted for his extraordinary knowledge of Rembrandt, whose deep interest in this book, while it was in process of preparation, was inspiring and helpful.

The Library of the Hebrew Union College, the Public Library and the Art Museum of Cincinnati were helpful in obtaining the pictures included in this volume. For illustrations 1, 8, 9, 40, 53 and 54, I am indebted to the Rembrandt editions of Bredius and Borenius published by the Phaidon Press in Oxford, to which I extend my heartfelt thanks.

Last but not least, I offer my thanks to The Jewish Publication Society of America and its Publication Committee.

FRANZ LANDSBERGER

Cincinnati
September, 1945

TABLE OF CONTENTS

LIST OF ILLUSTRATIONS

REMBRANDT, THE JEWS
AND THE BIBLE

I

REMBRANDT AND THE JEWS COME TO AMSTERDAM

IN THE year 1606 a son was born to a miller in the city of Leyden, in Holland. He was given the unusual name of Rembrandt. The family already counted a goodly number of children, all of whom grew up to be worthy citizens in their community. One of these became a baker, another a shoemaker. In his boyhood days Rembrandt stood out among his brethren as a young Joseph, the biblical Joseph whose adventures Rembrandt in later years delighted to portray. He was not an especially comely youngster — his rather fleshy nose lending a certain plumpness to his countenance — and one of his first biographers referred to his features as unattractive and plebeian (fig. 1).[1] What was manifest in the boy at an early period was his unusual and vivid intelligence. It was this that impelled his parents to send him to the Latin School, and, seven years later, to enroll him among the students of the University in the city of his birth.

In the Latin School the curriculum included — besides the usual subjects of mathematics, geography and history — courses in Latin, as its name implied. These courses provided not only translation, but the acquisition of Latin as a language to be spoken and written.

It was, of course, the language which, at that period, was the universal medium of scholarly intercourse throughout Christendom. Beyond this practical requirement, the knowledge of Latin opened a wide vista of classical culture and revealed a world of heroic deeds, wise thoughts, and poetic fantasies. All this was designed to make a deep impression upon the spirit of a sensitive and aspiring youth, and we find an outcome of these studies in the great number of pagan subjects taken from legendary, poetic and historic sources, which Rembrandt included in his works.

The School's emphasis on ancient culture was, however, subordinated to studies covering the Christian faith and ideals. Classes were opened with prayer, a chapter from the Bible was read every day, and the pupils joined in the singing of Psalms.[2] Later, at the University, there were more intensive studies in the realms of antiquity and of Christianity. It is probable that Rembrandt began, at this time, the study of Hebrew, a study that had formed for more than a century, since the awakening of humanistic interests, a feature of higher European culture. It became the fashion, in intellectual circles, to read the books of the Old Testament in the original text. Many even devoted themselves to a study of the medieval Jewish philosophers and the mysteries of the Cabala.

We have indicated that Rembrandt probably "began" the study of Hebrew, as his stay at the University covered only a short period. For at the time he entered upon his studies at the University there developed in him the consciousness of a new gift, that of reproducing accurately, with pen or brush, objects he saw about him. It is possible

4

that for a time both these interests were concurrently active; but before long the inclination toward a scholarly career grew ever weaker, while his desire to draw and paint grew steadily stronger. Soon he discontinued his University studies and was turned over to an apprenticeship under a local teacher of painting. Rembrandt was at this time only fourteen years of age, and the change in vocation played but a minor role. After the required three years of his apprenticeship had been concluded the boy was sent by his father to Amsterdam to have the advantage of more advanced studies under the tutorship of the distinguished painter, Pieter Lastman, a highly esteemed and widely cultured individual, who had even spent some time in Italy, that hallowed land of all artists since the days of the Renaissance.

For Rembrandt, himself, Italy held no lure. It appears that he never journeyed beyond the restricted boundaries of his native Holland.[3] For this reason he did not follow the period of his apprenticeship with the customary travel adventure, but returned from Amsterdam to his native city, establishing a studio in which his work met with prompt and gratifying recognition. A pupil even found his way to him, Gerard Dou, a youth of fifteen years, who was the first to take instruction from the twenty-three-year-old Rembrandt.

Matters progressed satisfactorily for several years, and would have continued to do so had Rembrandt possessed a conventional bourgeois spirit such as characterized this Gerard Dou, who throughout all his life, into old age, was content to paint his little, workman-

like, pedantic pictures, which brought him so satisfactory a recom-
pense that he never left his little town of Leyden. Rembrandt was
of a different temperament. He was ambitious and aspired to wider
horizons. He wanted to create works of art that should not be small
and meticulous and have their merits determined through the
medium of a magnifying glass. His desire was to produce works of a
stately and imposing character, so that to see them in proper per-
spective one would have to step back several paces from the can-
vases.[4] He wished to attain to such heights as a painter that he
might be surrounded by wealth and splendor, and have not only
one but a great number of pupils. Such a dream, if it were to be
realized at all in a country like Holland, required for its locale a
capital city, a place like Amsterdam, which provided opportunities
which he had probably recognized in the days of his studies with
Pieter Lastman.

Amsterdam at that period was a city which, owing to its favorable
location as a seaport, was destined to become of great commercial
importance. It formed a highroad for the transportation of goods
from the countries of southern Europe to the northern lands, and
from those of the north to southern ports. Its far-flung channels of
trade extended across the ocean to the new world, to America. In
brief, the metropolis had in these years developed into the foremost
commercial port of Europe.

In his early youth, Rembrandt had already possessed the ability
to create on his canvas an exact reproduction of the human face.
This gift was especially esteemed in Amsterdam. It is a recognized

6

trait of successful persons who have risen rapidly to affluence to want their portraits painted, and to transmit such evidences of their existence to their descendants. The successful burghers of Amsterdam shared this human propensity. On his occasional visits to the city requests from one person or another to paint such portraits had probably been made to the young Rembrandt. Now, however, a more important commission reached him. It was to execute a large group painting, representing a body of physicians assembled about their instructor, the celebrated Professor Tulp, for a lesson in anatomy. This commission necessitated an extended stay in Amsterdam, and Rembrandt realized that this might provide a springboard for permanent residence in the great city.

Success favored his undertaking. The group painting of the physicians revealed the virtuosity of the artist. His fame spread rapidly, and commissions for portraits poured in upon him. Even Prince Henry Frederick of Orange, the Stadtholder of the country, manifested his interest and requested him to execute a cycle of paintings depicting scenes from the Passion of Christ. Many pupils gathered about him, and in these new activities his early classical studies doubtless stood him in good stead. He who had been so assiduous a student in the Latin School and in the University possessed the rare quality of being able to impart his ideas readily to others.

A woman soon came to share his life, Saskia van Uylenburgh. She was not of the humble station he himself occupied, but was a woman of unusual charm, endowed with wealth, and a member of one of the best families of Holland. She must have seemed to the somewhat uncouth Rembrandt like a princess, and he adorned her with beautiful clothes and pearls. He purchased a palatial residence (fig. 2), which he not only filled with pupils, but also with costly materials, ornaments, corals, weapons, and works of art. Amsterdam, in addition to its prominence as a great commercial capital, had grown to be the foremost art dealers' center of Europe, and afforded a constant temptation to visitors in the metropolis to carry home with them some of the treasures so attractively displayed. Inasmuch as Rembrandt had never visited Italy, he was thus enabled to find in Amsterdam, and even to acquire, masterpieces of Italian art, to appraise their worth, and to make a study of the magic employed by their creators, a magic that had given to these works so pre-eminent a place in the art-loving circles of Europe.

Rembrandt's success and good fortune faced only one drawback. They did not last. Saskia's children died in early youth, and only one son, Titus, lived to maturity. Saskia herself, reared, as was Rembrandt, in a small, provincial town, soon succumbed under the unaccustomed strain and turmoil of metropolitan existence, and died while still young. Rembrandt's earnings, large as they were, did not suffice for his luxurious manner of living. He possessed little talent in financial affairs. When, at one or another of the various public sales of paintings, he wished to acquire a work of art, he started by making bids that were so extravagantly high that he provoked annoyance among competing purchasers. To justify his

8

2.   Rembrandt's House in the Jewish Quarter of Amsterdam.

actions he would protest that he acted as he did in order to emphasize the prestige of his profession. The true reason was, doubtless, that the sight of a great work of art brought about an emotional agitation causing him to lose control of his better judgment.

In addition to this unbridled collector's passion there was another untoward activity. Commercial speculation had grown rife in Amsterdam, and Rembrandt became involved in some rather risky financial adventures, which proved unsuccessful, resulting in serious losses. He was compelled to borrow money at high rates of interest, plunging into ever greater indebtedness. When his creditors finally lost patience with him, Rembrandt was forced into bankruptcy. His splendid residence was sold, and his treasures of art and curios were disposed of at a great sacrifice and scattered to the wind.

He found solace for his misfortunes in the love of a young woman, Henrickje Stoffels. She was not a "princess," like Saskia, but, like himself, a child of the people, who had entered his household as a servant. But she was in every way devoted to the master and was ready to serve him in work or in affection, as a model or as a comrade, in the serious or lighter phases of existence. Following Rembrandt's financial debacle, she, together with his son, Titus, at that time nineteen years old, established an art emporium, devoted in the main to the sale of Rembrandt's own paintings and etchings. In this undertaking Rembrandt's participation was that of a paid employee. By this method the proceeds of the business were withheld from the grasp of creditors and the earnings of Henrickje and of his son in

10

the venture were doubtless much better conserved than if they had been controlled by the head of the house.

The artist undoubtedly adjusted himself to these circumscribed conditions of life without reluctance.[5] It is true that he had lost many of his contacts with the fashionable world; but this was not a matter of much concern to him as he was thereby relieved of many obligations and was enabled to devote himself unreservedly to his art, in which he attained an ever increasing mastery. A few of his friends remained loyal to him; a few pupils continued their studies with him; and, occasionally, there were some commissions for portraits. It was not long, moreover, before recognition of the high quality of his work penetrated to foreign lands — notably to England and Italy.

Of course, no one in those years imagined that this painter would at a later day come to be regarded as Holland's greatest artist; yes, perhaps, the greatest in all of Europe. When he died, in 1669, he was given a very modest burial. "In this vast city," wrote the French philosopher Descartes, who had resided in Amsterdam shortly before this time, "in this vast city, where I am the only man not engaged in trade, everyone is so actively occupied in money-making, that I might spend my whole life in complete solitude."[6] It was so, too, with the aging Rembrandt. The great city had for a time acclaimed and exalted him, but had then pursued the noisy tenor of its way as though no comet had swept across its sky.

A few years before Rembrandt's birth a small group of refugees — a peculiar people — had come to Holland. They came from Portugal and outwardly were members of the Catholic faith, as were all the inhabitants of the Iberian Peninsula. But deep within their hearts they cherished the memory of a more ancient faith, a faith they had been compelled to abjure about a hundred years before — their Judaism. The ancestors of the greater number of these Portuguese refugees had resided in Spain, whence they had been driven in 1492, since which time they had found asylum in Portugal. It was not long, however, before the virus of Spanish intolerance spread into Portugal, and its manifestations became even more violent than had been the case in Spain. The Jews had simply been expelled from the latter country. In Portugal, however, they were subjected to cruel and relentless persecutions. Their children, of from four to fourteen years of age, were torn from their arms and forcibly compelled to accept the Christian faith. The parents were threatened with enslavement if they refused to abjure their former belief.

A considerable number yielded to this coercion and adjusted their outward lives to the conditions imposed upon them, becoming successful and well-to-do members of their communities. They were bankers and merchants; they practiced medicine, secured commissions as military officers, and some even entered the priesthood. Others achieved fame as scholars and poets. Of interest in this connection is the story of Uriel d'Acosta, who wrote in his autobiography: "I was born in Portugal, in the city that bears this name, generally referred to as 'Porto.' My parents belonged to the nobility (*ex ordine nobilium*). They traced their origin to the Jewish race, the members of which had been compelled to adopt the Christian faith in former years. My father was a believing Christian and man of rigid honor, who laid great store upon social rank and condition. In this home I was reared in keeping with the standing of the family. There was no scarcity of servitors, and in our stables there was a noble Spanish steed for equestrian practice, to which my father was much devoted, while I, from my early years, followed his example." Uriel d'Acosta was destined for the priesthood. He matriculated at the University of Coimbra, and received an appointment as bursar of a collegiate church. At this time he began to grow skeptical regarding some of the dogmas of Christianity, and there awoke in him a remembrance of the Jewish faith of his forebears. As many others had done before his day, he secretly left Portugal in the year 1615 and journeyed to Amsterdam, where he openly avowed his return to the Jewish fold.

We are here presented with a peculiar case. The father was a devout and observant Catholic; and the son, a Catholic church official, had become disaffected with the tenets of his faith. In most cases those who had left their Judaism never became true Christians. They were only crypto-Jews — Marranos, "swine," as they were contemptuously designated by the Christians. These Marranos lived in a continual state of danger. Despite their wealth and the high places they occupied in the community, perhaps, in fact, due to the envy provoked by the prominence they attained, they were compelled to be continually conscious of the menace of the Inquisition, and were keen to avoid any embroilment that would lead them into its meshes. Once caught in this web they were as good as lost, and their fate was incarceration in dungeons or death at the stake.

It became known to these Marranos that a small country existed in northern Europe where they would be made welcome without being required to deny adherence to their ancient faith.

What basis had the Jews for reliance on this promise of tolerance? Had not the people of Holland, during the Middle Ages, even as had the English, the French and the Germans, massacred or expelled their coreligionists in these countries, regarding them as enemies of their faith and a menace to their welfare? Such persecutions had, in fact, occurred. But in the 16th century the newly propagated message of Martin Luther had spread throughout this land, the inhabitants of which had accepted the tenets of the Reformation in its Calvinist form. It was just at this time that Holland experienced the misfortune, through the accident of heritage, of being subjected to the political yoke of an intensely Catholic country, this very Spain that had ordered the Jews expelled from its territory. The people in Holland now apprehended in their own persons the meaning of religious persecution. In a mighty national uprising they succeeded in freeing themselves from the rule of the foreign oppressor. In 1579 the northern provinces assembled in Utrecht to form a union, and they there and then made solemn declaration that their liberated country should hold aloft the standard of religious tolerance. Every citizen "should be accorded freedom of worship and no one should be molested on account of his belief."

These reverberations, heralding a new promise of toleration, had reached the ears of the wealthy but terror-stricken Marranos of the Iberian Peninsula, and had induced them, at first as scattered individuals and later in ever increasing numbers, to emigrate to this new land of liberty where they could openly avow their Jewish faith. The greater number of these refugees established themselves in the largest city of Holland, in Amsterdam, where, in the middle of the 17th century, they numbered about 400 families.

The Amsterdam Christians, after some preliminary hesitation, having at first regarded the new arrivals as old Catholics rather than as new Jews, manifested no opposition to the newcomers. These Jews were not by any means a group of poverty-stricken refugees such as the Nazi terror has in recent years driven from Germany into other lands; they were, on the contrary, persons of property with a variety of means at their disposal in the event of a favorable outcome to their hopes of settlement in the northern country. And the Hollanders were not only a pious folk who followed the precepts of love for one's fellowmen in a literal sense; they were also a practical people who realized the importance to their material and commercial welfare of the influx of large batches of capital.

Thus there was the practical consideration, the probability, namely, that the Jews of the Iberian Peninsula — the Sephardim — were likely to prove of advantage to the Hollanders in furthering

15

the expansion of their commerce in foreign lands. Following the expulsion from Spain in 1492, and some years later from Portugal, Sephardi Jews migrated to Italy, to southern France, to Turkey, to provinces in Northern Africa and to sections of Asia, and opened new channels of trade among these countries. If they now established a new basis of activity in Holland, they were likely to include it in the net of their far-flung operations. Thereafter the Jews did, in fact, manifest a lively interest in the development of new routes of trade which led from Holland to the marts of the East Indies and America. Ultimately they also played a leading role as bankers on the Amsterdam Bourse. For these reasons the relations existing between the Jews and the Hollanders in the 17th century were based not alone upon personal amity, but upon mutual interests that developed steadily in extent and importance. A Christian observer, Jacques Basnage, who early in the 18th century published a history of the Jewish people, wrote the following description of the prominent place occupied by the Jews in Holland: "Of all the states of Europe there is not one in which the Jews live more peaceably than in Holland. They acquire wealth through trade, and owing to the friendly attitude of the Government are secure in their standing and possessions."[7]

To live in peace and without fear was surely an ideal condition for a people who had throughout the centuries been hounded from place to place.

Although the privileges accorded the Jews who streamed into Holland were not quite so generous as one might have expected,

16

especially in the early days of their coming, they touched upon matters that gave to these victims of ruthless persecution a new consciousness of human dignity. For one thing, they were relieved of the humiliating requirement of wearing upon their garments the symbols that stamped them as pariahs. Nor were they now compelled to herd into such restricted quarters as ghettos, in which they had formerly been locked at nightfall, as though they were a species of wild and dangerous animal that had to be confined in cages. If the Jews neglected to avail themselves of this opportunity, and selected as their place of residence a southern section of Amsterdam, it was entirely due to their own volition and not because of any compulsion. Regardless of the cruel injustice under which they had suffered in Spain and Portugal, they continued using the language of these countries, and in this practice were held together more closely than they were with their Dutch neighbors. The daily attendance at synagogue services, too, made it desirable to establish their homes in the vicinity of these places of worship. But, as we have pointed out, this residential quarter was in no sense a ghetto, and many Christians had their homes in the same district of the city. Among these were a few painters, and we shall find later that Rembrandt, too, resided in this part of the town.[8]

Holland, in 1657, declared these immigrant Sephardim to be "subjects and residents of the United Netherlands," and this citizenship accorded them, in the first place, protection while travelling in foreign countries. It gave to them all the treaty-rights the Hollanders had established for themselves. It is true that in this Act of Recognition the Jews were not referred to as Hollanders, but were described as members of the "Jewish Nation." This designation indicated that their inclusion with the Hollanders on a plane of equality was not complete. They were not permitted, for one thing, to enter into amatory or marital relations with Christians. Nor were they allowed to employ Christians as domestic servants. The reasons for these restrictions were not racial, but were based upon a religious separateness. It was feared that possible conversions might emanate from Jewish teachings, and, as a matter of fact, there were at that time several instances of Christian apostasy due to the influence of Jewish ideas.[9]

Certain political rights were also withheld from the Jews. All municipal and provincial offices were reserved for Hollanders. There were restrictions in the admission of Jews to the guilds, these organizations being based not only upon specific trade interests, but also upon religious principles. Children of Jews were not admitted to the schools; these, too, as we recall in the case of the Latin School attended by Rembrandt, were largely devoted to religious instruction.

These restrictions, however, proved of little importance to the Jews. They were unhindered in their activities as shipowners, importers and exporters of commodities, brokers, agents, physicians, and lawyers. If they desired to take up some handicraft, they could have their own masters instruct their children in its rudiments. At any rate, this latter type of activity played a minor role in the social structure of their existence.

18

The Jews would not have enrolled their children in Christian schools, in any event, even had it been permitted, for their own methods of education provided, to an even greater degree than those of the Christians, instruction in the history and tenets of their faith. For this reason they established their own elementary and high schools, in the curricula of which, as had been the case in the Middle Ages, all knowledge centered about a profound comprehension of the teachings of their sacred writings. There was, for example, the school known as *Ets Hayyim,* "Tree of Life," divided into seven classes, exactly as had been the Latin School which Rembrandt had attended in Leyden. In the first class instruction was given in Hebrew letters and the vowel-signs; in the second, the reading of the Pentateuch; in the third, the time was devoted to translating the Five Books of Moses into Spanish; in the fourth, the Books of the Prophets formed the basis of study; and in the fifth, the class took up the Commentary on the Pentateuch by Rashi, the great scholar of the Middle Ages. The last two classes were devoted to the study of the Talmud.

The textbooks for the required studies were printed on their own presses, and before long they attained a reputation that created a demand for them in all the Jewries of Europe. In the latter half of the 17th century, one of these Jewish printers, Joseph Athias, succeeded in extending his clientele into Christian circles, and in an introduction to a Hebrew-Yiddish Bible, published in 1686, he proudly asserted: "For several years I myself printed more than a million Bibles for distribution in England and Scotland, and in those countries there is not a plowboy or a servant girl who does not possess one." This same Athias was even admitted to membership in the Booksellers' Guild. There were other individual cases in which the restrictions under which the Jews of Amsterdam labored were modified.

The wealth acquired by the Sephardi Jews enabled them to construct imposing synagogues and adorn them with splendid and ornate ritualistic appointments. It also provided them with the means for building stately residences, the wearing of rich habiliments and precious jewels, and adopting a sumptuous manner of living, which included, as we shall have occasion to note, the acquisition of works of art. The drawing of a circumcision by a Dutch artist (fig.3) provides an example of their manner of life, as depicted by the elaborately canopied four-poster bed in which the young mother is resting, and the exquisitely carved doorway, on which are carved in Hebrew letters the words: "Blessed shalt thou be when thou comest in, and blessed shalt thou be when thou goest out." Their riches, moreover, also afforded scope to their natural charitable impulses, innate in the Jewish character throughout the ages. Not only were the needy provided for, so that there were no beggars among them, but funds were made available in the shape of loans on which no interest charges were exacted. Dowries were established for daughters of poor parents, as well as for orphans for whom desirable marriages were arranged, and societies were organized for the care of the sick and for the proper burial of the dead.

With the same zeal, however, with which the Sephardi Jews

3. Romeyn de Hooghe, "A Circumcision in a Dutch Home." Drawing.

devoted themselves to caring for the needs of the poor and unfortunate, they opposed those among them who attacked the observances of the rituals of their faith. Woe unto the Jew who failed
to comply with the dietary laws or who was found guilty of desecrat-
ing the Sabbath, or who expressed skepticism in the established tenets
of their religion, or cast doubt, for example, upon belief in personal
immortality, and gave expression to such infidelity in speech or by
the written word! Such a one would be haled before the officials of
the congregation, and, in the event of stubborn persistence in his
recalcitrance, be severely disciplined. He would be subjected to
either the Minor Ban, which involved suspension from the congregation for a period of thirty days, or the Major Ban would be pronounced against him, which enjoined any Jew, even the nearest
relative of the offender, from holding conversation with him or giving
him shelter in his home. "In accordance with the judgment of the
angels" — so read the text of this excommunication — "and in
accordance with the pronouncements of the saints, with the consent of God, blessed be He, and with the consent of all the Holy
Congregation, in front of the Holy Scrolls with the six-hundred-and-
thirteen precepts which are written therein, we excommunicate,
expel, curse, and damn — — with the excommunication with
which Joshua banned Jericho, with the curse with which Elisha
cursed the boys, and with all the curses which are written in the
Law. Cursed be he by day and cursed be he by night; cursed be
he when he lieth down, and cursed be he when he riseth up; cursed
be he when he goeth out, and cursed be he when he cometh in.

22

May the Lord never pardon him; may the anger and wrath of the Lord rage against this man, and bring upon him all the curses which are written in the Book of the Law . . . ."

These are surely no expressions of amity and fall far short of the spirit of tolerance that had been manifested towards the Jews by the people of Holland. In extenuation it may be pointed out that what we term tolerance was generally in those days an attitude adopted towards the faith of the stranger, but not to any defection from one's own religious beliefs. The Calvinists, too, practiced a rigid ecclesiastical regimentation, and applied the stern discipline of excommunication against any apostate. It must also be remembered that these refugees had just returned to a consciousness and practice of their ancestral faith, and were proud to have their Amsterdam referred to as the New Jerusalem. A bulwark such as this must, they felt, be defended by every available means. At any rate, such bans and excommunications could not be compared with the martyrdom to which the Inquisition had subjected its victims.

It was unfortunate that this Major Ban should have been invoked against the foremost Jewish thinker of Holland in the 17th century, Baruch Spinoza. When he died, in 1677, after having passed his last years among Christian friends, the Jews of Amsterdam were as little aware that they had ejected from their midst one of the immortals of their people, as were the Hollanders, in 1669, that they had lost one of the world's greatest artists, a genius whose eminence would one day be acclaimed throughout the world.

While the Jews who had come to Holland from the Iberian

Peninsula constituted, in Rembrandt's time, the most important element of Amsterdam's Jewish community, they were not the only members of the ancient faith who had found asylum in this city. For in the early years of the 17th century anti-Jewish outbreaks and pogroms in Frankfort-on-the-Main and Worms had, doubtless, driven many a refugee to this outpost of liberty. Others, too, may have come here to escape the devastations of the Thirty Years' War. These German Jews — the Ashkenazim — represented, in comparison with the proud and well-to-do Sephardim, a plebeian class. They dealt in provisions and secondhand goods. They worked as shoemakers and tailors or occupied places as employees in the Sephardi-controlled establishments. At a later period some individuals came with small stocks of jewelry or with slight financial means. Others managed to achieve a competence under the existing favorable conditions. In this way, the German group gradually attained a position of consequence.

In their attendance at religious services they were, at first, guests of the Sephardim. But inasmuch as their synagogue ritual differed in many details from that of the Sephardim, and as they spoke a different language, Yiddish, an idiom that had been developed from the German of the Middle Ages, they soon established a congregational life of their own. They built their own houses of worship and instituted their own elementary and high schools, intermarried only among themselves, and indicated by the purchase of their own burial grounds that even in death they were determined to retain their separateness. As a matter of course, the Sephardim

24

would not have permitted any such intermingling. They regarded themselves as a nobler race and manifested this sense of superiority in their public and private lives, although the Ashkenazim possessed a greater fund of general and religious learning. In Basnage's above-mentioned history of the Jews, the author, commenting upon the relations existing between the Ashkenazi and Sephardi Jews, wrote: "They are divided in matters of some of their ceremonial observances, and hate one another as though the essentials of their religion were involved." This may be somewhat of an exaggeration, but there can be no doubt that strained relations existed between the two factions.

A third group of Jews filtered into Holland after the year 1648. These came from Poland. They, too, were Ashkenazim, who had fled from Germany toward the east at the time of the bloody persecutions of the Middle Ages. Now, pogroms had broken out in Poland, the victims of which were counted in the tens of thousands. Only a few of those who survived these massacres had been able to escape and find refuge in their old homeland, and some of these managed to get as far as Holland. In this country their numbers were quickly augmented. In like manner as the German Jews had at first enjoyed the hospitality of the Sephardim, so now the Polish Jews attached themselves to their German coreligionists. But they, too, had in the course of the centuries developed individual customs and now strove toward an autonomous existence, establishing their own synagogues and burial grounds.

This was the picture of Jewish life in Holland, especially in

Amsterdam, presenting no uniformity as a communal body, but revealing distinctive diversities in speech, attire and customs. For an attentive observer, such as Rembrandt, the Jews in their picturesque variety must have held a peculiar interest.

II

REMBRANDT'S PORTRAITS OF JEWS

BEFORE approaching the relations that grew up between Rembrandt and the Jews of Holland, a few words must be said about the place occupied by the painter's art in his day, for only in this way can a comprehensive understanding of these relations be reached. Painting at that time was subject to a line of thought that had governed this form of art for centuries, namely, a faithful reproduction of nature on the part of the artist. It might appear to us that such a goal should be a matter of course; but this had been by no means the case. In the Middle Ages the art of painting held, as its highest aim, the representation of Christian teachings; Nature was utilized only to the degree to which it was absolutely necessary in connection with carrying out this theological purpose.

The new epoch had begun when the attenuated, incorporeal figures of the saints, with their rigid, ascetic physiognomies, vanished, and their places were taken by figures that resembled real human beings, beings that could laugh and weep. And the beginning of the new epoch had been shown also in the gradual disappearance of the gilded backgrounds against which these holy figures had been placed and the introduction in their stead of lovely landscapes, with valleys, hills, clouds, and rivers.

This tendency had already become evident in the later Middle Ages; it reached its highest flowering in the 15th and 16th centuries, the period of the Renaissance. In the paintings of the Renaissance the artists had striven to represent the aspects of Nature in all their truth as well as in their beauty. The Italian artist, Leone Battista Alberti, who flourished at that time, has given expression to this aim of the artist in the following words: "We will select the subjects of our paintings from the realm of Nature and we will always choose those that are the most beautiful."[10]

The representation of Nature implied in that age an exact reproduction of every detail of the object selected by the artist. In painting a meadow every blade of grass and every flower was carefully depicted; and in picturing the human form, each separate member of the body, every muscle and every vein was shown. If it was a face, the artist gave the exact expression of the sitter's eyes, and contours of the nose and the mouth. In this way there was obtained, for the first time since Antiquity, an actual representation of the individual: in other words, a portrait.

But in every instance an equal emphasis was placed upon beauty. Preference was given to the portrayal of youthful or gracefully developed figures, the noble and the stately; while the reproduction of the aged, the unattractive, the sickly, so far as possible, was sedulously avoided. The outlines of the figures, as they were revealed against the background of the painting, had to be graceful and flowing; every color was given a radiance, and, where several were combined, they were harmoniously blended.

In the period immediately following, the Baroque, which reached its apogee in Rembrandt's time, the depiction of Nature in the realm of artistic creation made distinct strides. The art of individual portraiture, for instance, attained greater perfection. In the portraits painted by a Velasquez, Frans Hals or Rembrandt, one meets with physiognomies of such vivid character that one has the impression of having known the original in the living flesh. Though these faces might be old or homely, or the individuals bear the marks of poverty or be shabbily attired, they were no less welcome to the painter. They were not now pictured with such accurate precision that every detail could be determined. Greater attention, rather, was directed to the play of light and shade in art creations. Already in the time of the Renaissance the relation of light and shade in painting had been introduced, but only for the purpose of providing a more vivid modelling of the figures and sharper clarifying of their shape. Now, however, the principle of light and shade entered the lists at the expense of distinctness. A brilliant light lent vividness to certain parts, while a deep shadow absorbed other phases of the picture. In the drawings and etchings of this period an outline was suddenly disrupted, at a high point of lighting, while in other parts of the picture the outline was submerged in darkness.

The color, too, was affected by the new conditions. At one place it almost faded into the shadow, while in another it was irradiated, as from the flare of a lighted torch, to glow with an even greater brilliance against the dark.

In any event, the effect of beauty was not lost sight of in the

29

Baroque, being, however, no longer dependent upon the subjects chosen, nor their form and color, but consequent upon the artistic manner in which the principle of the application of light and shade lit up or darkened the painting.

In this phase of Baroque painting Rembrandt played an important and significant role. He had, in a greater degree than almost any other contemporary artist, striven to achieve an imitation of Nature in all its manifestations; he had even found them interesting and appealing when they took the form of the decrepit, the frail, the ragged or the ailing, and he, more than others, poured over this world the enchantment of light and the glow of color.

Rembrandt, in his early years in Leyden, probably had never seen a Jew, although he had, doubtless, come across some members of this people during his first stay in Amsterdam, where he spent the last six months of his apprenticeship. Upon his return to Leyden he painted some scenes of biblical life, the figures in which reveal no distinctly Jewish features. An exception, however, is to be found in a picture of Judas, painted in 1629 (fig. 4).[11] Here Rembrandt shows the Apostle at the moment he is returning to the High Priest and the Elders the thirty pieces of silver he had received for the betrayal of Jesus, saying: "I have sinned in that I have betrayed the innocent blood," and being repulsed with the words: "What is that to us? See thou to that." Whereupon Judas "cast down the pieces of silver in the Temple and departed, and went and hanged himself" (Matthew 27.3–5).

4. Rembrandt, "Judas Returning the Thirty Pieces of Silver." Painting.

To the extent that one may sound the depths of Rembrandt's mental attitude in a single instance, such as is provided by this painting, it may be analyzed as follows: He shared the hatred of the centuries against Judas, and it is not improbable that he sympathized with the then generally prevailing opinion that the Jew was capable of every despicable action. This attitude toward the Jew found constant expression throughout the Christian world. In Shakespeare's *Merchant of Venice*, written about the year 1600, only shortly before Rembrandt's time, the poet had created an immortal figure of the despised Jew. But Rembrandt, in this painting, stepped beyond the narrower confines of the spirit of hatred. It was not the betrayal, but the deep sense of remorse in Judas's consciousness of his action that appeared to the painter as significant. For this reason, although he accentuated the repulsiveness of Judas's appearance, the manner in which he depicted the Apostle as throwing first the pieces of silver and then himself upon the ground, wringing his hands in his despair, portrayed something profoundly touching.

The painting confirms, at the same time, our previous conjecture that Rembrandt had acquired some rudiments of Hebrew during his stay at the University in Leyden. The standing figure with the high headgear is draped in a mantle adorned with several letters of the Hebrew alphabet. Then, too, there is shown in front of the seated figure, a large volume upon the open pages of which some lines of writing are faintly discernible. One can glimpse at the extreme top a few Hebrew letters (see fig. 5). A fold at the upper corner of the page obliterates several letters, but those that are

5. Detail of Figure 4.

distinguishable suggest the words לדעותן ומ[צ]ותך: "To know Thy Law." We are unable here to go beyond a conjecture,[12] but one thing is certain: Rembrandt revealed in this painting, as well as in later ones, an inclination toward the use of Hebrew letters. It is possible that he was attracted by their aesthetic outlines, their regularity and strength — a strength that, however, is not without grace.

Rembrandt, in 1631 or 1632, when he removed to Amsterdam, made his home with Hendrik Uylenburgh, a dealer in works of art, in the *Breestraat*, the present day *Jodenbrestraat*, a section of the city that had been selected as a residential quarter by the Jews. Later, in 1639, when the artist was in a position to purchase a home for himself, he again selected a house in the *Breestraat*, an imposing three-story building, in the style of the Renaissance, that is still in existence and is maintained as a Rembrandt Memorial (fig. 2). Among his nearest neighbors in this street were the Jews Daniel Pinto, Salvador Rodriguez and Jacob Belmonte, while on the opposite side of the street was the residence of Rabbi Manasseh ben Israel. In this home of his, Rembrandt harbored his extensive valuable collections. Here he gave instruction to his numerous pupils. But, here, too, he experienced the tragedy of his bankruptcy, which compelled him, in 1658, to sell his house and find refuge, during the last ten or eleven years of his life, in another quarter of the city. During the longest period of his residence in Amsterdam, however, Rembrandt had lived in close proximity to the Jews of the town.

To what extent this physical proximity influenced a more intimate spiritual relation cannot be determined by any existing records. The assertion is often made in otherwise reliable biographical works on Rembrandt that he was a close friend of Rabbi Manasseh ben Israel. While this was not unlikely, there is no evidence to this effect. We know only that Rembrandt made a portrait and etching of the distinguished rabbi, and that he furnished illustrations for one of the latter's books; these illustrations, however, seem never to have been published; in any event, they have been replaced by other pictures.

It is, in this connection, a pleasant conjecture that Ephraim Bonus, the well-known Jewish physician and poet, had been an acquaintance of Rembrandt's or had, at any rate, professional relations with him and his family. But all that we know with certainty is that Rembrandt painted his portrait and made an etching of him; this may have simply been in performance of a commission.

On one occasion Rembrandt had a serious dispute with a Jewish client, one Diego d'Andrada, who had commissioned him to paint a portrait. This d'Andrada had, in 1654, given an order to Rembrandt for a picture of a young woman and had made a partial payment of 75 guldens. When the portrait was finished and delivered, d'Andrada refused to accept it, demanding that the painter make certain alterations or cancel the order. Rembrandt contended that full payment be made before the alterations or that payment of the money still due for the work be guaranteed, and then made a counter-proposal to submit the decision as to the disputed resemblance of the portrait with its subject to the officials of the Guild of Painters, agreeing to abide by their judgment and alter the painting or leave it as it was. Disputes of this nature were also experienced by Rembrandt with some of his Christian clients, and we have no reason to believe that a single instance of this kind should have aroused any anti-Semitic sentiments in him. Everything we know of him points to the contrary and suggests that he was a friend of the Jews; although this conclusion is based upon conjecture and not upon any available evidence.

The above specified portraits of Manasseh ben Israel, Dr. Bonus and the daughter of Diego d'Andrada afford evidence of the relationship existing between Rembrandt and the Jews. He was their painter; not the only one, of course, for we know that a number of Dutch artists executed portraits of Jews in the 17th century: William Cornelisz Duyster, Jan Lievens, Nicolaes Maes, Aart de Gelder, Jacob Toorenvliet, Aernout Nagtegaal, Adrian van der Werff and others. But the work of none of these includes so large a number of Jewish portraits as does Rembrandt's. Undoubtedly he had frequent dealings with them.

It must be said that it is not possible to establish with any degree of certainty that every one of the portraits which have been thought to be those of Jews actually represented Jewish individuals. The names of the sitters have in many cases been lost. Their apparel does not provide a conclusive indication, as it is similar to that worn by the Hollanders. So far as the features are concerned, they are by no means always dependable. The more or less melancholy, tired expression which characterizes many Jewish physiognomies is found also in the Christian faces painted by Rembrandt, especially in his later period. It undoubtedly reflects the spiritual disposition of the painter. It is for this reason that in the Rembrandt albums one portrait may be designated, without further identification, as that of "a man," while another as that of "a Jew," the decision in the matter being left to the judgment of the beholder. But even under the most careful examination the Jewish paintings are found to form an important part of Rembrandt's productivity. Abraham Bredius, the renowned authority on Rembrandt, who assembled the paintings of the master in a handy volume, included in his book — apart from the portraits of Rembrandt himself and the members of his family — about two hundred pictures of men. Of this number he designated thirty-seven, or about one-fifth, as being the portraits of Jews. If it is borne in mind that in Rembrandt's time the Jews numbered only about one per cent of the total population of Amsterdam, the proportion represented by this element reaches a high level.

Rembrandt's Jewish portraits were begun by him immediately after his removal to Amsterdam,[13] and continued with undiminished ardor to form part of his work throughout his entire career. We find herein a noticeable difference in his attitude toward the painting of non-Jewish portraits. Here, his greatest productivity occurred in the early period, when the painter was winning a rapid popularity by his indefatigable application. The marriage to Saskia, and the consequent advantageous social connections, doubtless, extended his opportunities of securing commissions for portraits. With the early

37

death of his wife, the artist relaxed into a lonesome, unsocial existence and at the same time acquired a more intensive artistic consciousness. Orders for portraits held little interest for him unless they provided full play to his artistic impulses. It is, doubtless, to this later period of his activities that the following reference by an early biographer of the artist, the Italian Baldinucci, applies: "He could have painted a large number of portraits owing to his great prestige ... but after it became generally known that whoever desired to have his portrait done by him would be compelled to sit to the painter for periods of two or three months, there were few who gave him commissions."

So far as the Jews were concerned, they made no objection to the length of time required by Rembrandt for the completion of their portraits. They were steadfast in their loyalty to the master throughout all his life, and this loyalty was rewarded in the creation by Rembrandt when he was in the fifties, his ripest years, of a number of his greatest portrait paintings.

All these portraits, in that they were commissioned by the Jews and for them, are representative of the Sephardim; due, in the main, to the fact that they were more affluent than their Ashkenazi brethren. Then, too, their attitude toward portraiture was different. Both were pious Jews, and as such were subject to the inhibition of the Second Commandment: "Thou shalt not make unto thee a graven image, nor any manner of likeness of anything that is in heaven above, or that is in the earth beneath, or that is in the water under the earth: thou shalt not bow down unto them nor serve them."

In the Middle Ages this Commandment was apprehended in its

38

definitely rigorous sense. Decorations in the synagogues were restricted to plants and animals, and only in the handwritten manuscripts were human figures included, as there was no idol worship to be feared in them.

In Italy, at the time of the Renaissance, the Jews adopted a wider latitude: the prevailing love of portraiture in this epoch exerting its widespread influence upon them. There is in existence an interesting pronouncement by the well-known Rabbi Leone da Modena (1571–1648), who in his work on Hebrew rites emphasized the inhibition of the Jews concerning graven images, but he appended in a somewhat compliant tone: "But in Italy there are many who have freed themselves from this restriction and have paintings and portraits in their homes, although avoiding works of sculpture, both in relief and in the round."[14] Works of sculpture were thus precluded, inasmuch as the biblical prohibition was specifically directed against plastic representations of the Deity.[15]

We are unacquainted with the artistic mores of the Jews in Spain and Portugal prior to the edicts of expulsion, or with the attitude maintained by the Marranos who remained in those countries, but we have every reason to believe that the latter freely acquiesced in the general love of the prevailing pictorial adornments. For they were living as Christians among Christians and were constantly anxious to avoid giving any ground for suspicion. They would, doubtless, for this reason alone, have adorned their homes in exactly the same fashion as did their neighbors. When they subsequently emigrated to other lands, they, in all probability, retained these

39

habits, inasmuch as they had lost the consciousness of their dereliction. This may afford the readiest explanation of the fact that the youthful Baruch Spinoza, for instance, while still a devout adherent of Jewish orthodoxy, made portrait drawings in carbon and ink;[16] that Ephraim Bonus, who was not only a physician but a writer of religious poetry, sat to Rembrandt for his portrait, or that even a Rabbi, Manasseh ben Israel, found no impropriety in a similar acquiescence.

The Ashkenazim, however, had an entirely different approach to this subject. Their lives, during the Renaissance, and even into the 18th century, had been much more isolated from their Christian fellow-citizens than had been those of the Italian Jews or the Marranos of the Iberian Peninsula, and they were, in consequence, more closely attached to their traditions. Their residence in Holland effected no change in this attitude. When the Rabbi of the Amsterdam Ashkenazi congregation, Zebi Ashkenazi, went to London in the winter of 1714–15, his admirers, probably Sephardim, desiring to have his portrait painted, were compelled to resort to subterfuge and have the painting made from a room adjoining that occupied by the Rabbi. He would never have given his consent to such a portrait.

It is evident, from the foregoing, that Rembrandt could not have received any commissions from the Ashkenazi Jews of Amsterdam to paint their portraits. At the same time there are found in the works of Rembrandt Jewish faces that bear no resemblance to those of the Sephardim, but are distinctly of Ashkenazic type. In the

6. Rembrandt, "Portrait of a Jew." Painting.

Westberlin Museum there is a head of a young Jew, which, according to the style of the painting, belongs to the output of the '40s of the 17th century (fig. 6). He wears the small cap which the pious Jew never removes. The hair frames the entire face. The cheek bones are broad, lending a Slavic touch to the features. The lips are protruding, the expression careworn, as though the subject had experienced suffering. This may be a Polish Jew, one of those who had escaped the pogrom of 1648 and fled to Holland. This head, however, was not designed by Rembrandt as a portrait, but rather as a study, and we shall see later how Rembrandt used it in one of his paintings. These Ashkenazi Jews had, of course, not ordered any paintings, but evidently did not regard it as sinful to pose as models for artists, and they may have been suitably rewarded for such services.

This is true, also, of the painting known as "Old Man with Red Fur Cap in an Armchair," executed a few years later, and exhibited in the same Museum (fig. 7). Here the sketchiness of the treatment would indicate that the painter did not intend this work as a portrait. The Jewish model evidently seated himself in a chair at the request of the painter, and the artist transferred him to the canvas with rapid strokes of his brush with the apparent intention of utilizing the subject in a painting. This man, with his untrimmed beard, has the facial characteristics of an East European Jew, also indicated by the warm fur cap and the heavy garments, more appropriate to Eastern Europe than to the temperate climate of Holland.[17]

What would appear to have been designed rather as a portrait is the head of an old Jew in the Museum at Groningen, Holland,

7. Rembrandt, "Old Man with Red Fur Cap in an Armchair." Painting.

8.   Rembrandt, "Portrait of a Jew."   Painting.

9.   Rembrandt, "Ephraim Bonus."   Painting.

10. Rembrandt, "Ephraim Bonus." Etching.

painted in 1654. But this, too, may have been intended as the study of a head, apparently not a commission, and executed for sale to a possible purchaser (fig. 8). Here, too, the untrimmed beard frames the entire face, and the rolled earlocks — the *peot* — worn even to our own times by Jews of Eastern Europe, are shown in the painting.

When we contrast this portrait with that of Dr. Ephraim Bonus, painted a few years earlier (fig. 9), we recognize the distinct difference between a Sephardi and an Ashkenazi Jew. Bonus is a cavalier, who has arrayed himself in the fine apparel of the high social strata of his environment. He wears a tall hat with a wide, flowing brim. The thick wavy hair, probably a wig, covers the ears. The beard does not frame the entire face but starts at the upper lip and falls, carefully trimmed, over the chin. The white collar is pleated, and white cuffs encircle the sleeves. This black and white effect lends to the aspect of the physician, as it did to the Hollanders of that day, something at the same time simple and aristocratic. Nobility is also stamped upon the features of the man, revealing an earnestness of character, especially in the expression of the eyes, and a dignified control of the emotions. In the case of the Ashkenazi Jews, everything is, on the contrary, more animated and unconstrained: the hat, the eyes, the expressive lips, the loosely worn garments.

Rembrandt fashioned an etching based upon his portrait of Bonus (fig. 10), in which the impression on the plate reverses the left and right sides of the painting. In this work the high standing of so distinguished a physician is revealed by the addition of an elabo-

11.   Jan Lievens, "Ephraim Bonus."   Etching.

rately carved stairway. The physician is apparently depicted in this etching at the moment of leaving his residence at the call of a patient. The expression of the face is given a tinge of sorrow by a shadow that falls upon the right cheek, and there is a touch of sadness in his eyes. A man is here pictured for us who, because of the seriousness of his nature, looks with sympathetic eyes upon the sufferings of his fellowmen. The warm and compassionate temperament of the Jewish physician has rarely been given a finer expression than is revealed in this etching.

A contemporary of Rembrandt's, Jan Lievens, has also given us a portrait of this physician, made at a somewhat later period of his life (fig. 11), and it is interesting to compare this design with the work of Rembrandt. The subject is here presented seated upon a chair placed in front of an ornate column. The tall hat is removed, but not the little cap, under which is shown a wealth of flowing hair. The coat, adorned with numerous buttons, and the cloak falling from the physician's shoulder, are depicted in richer fashion than in the work of Rembrandt. But this emphasis on the splendor of the attire detracts in large measure from the facial portraiture. There is in Lievens' etching a mobile expression in the features caused by the light that plays upon the hair and about the beard, and also owing to the slanted pose of the face, whereas the Rembrandt portrait shows the subject in full face. It may be that Lievens' etching bears a more faithful resemblance to the original than does that of Rembrandt. But the latter discerns beyond the individual the species, and beyond the species the man. This is Ephraim Bonus;

49

12.   Rembrandt, "Manasseh ben Israel."   Etching.

this is the Jew who has experienced centuries of suffering; this is the man who faces and strives to plumb the insoluble mystery of human destiny.

The etching of Manasseh ben Israel which Rembrandt had made in 1636 (fig. 12), based, doubtless, upon a painted portrait that is no longer in existence,[18] does not reveal the same depth of expression as that shown in the Ephraim Bonus. The profound impression made by the great Rabbi upon those among whom he lived has been thus described by a contemporary writer: "He was of medium stature and inclined to be stout. He did not wear a wig, and his hair, gray long before his death, his fresh complexion and graceful attractive demeanor, the plain but presentable dress, induced an attitude of reverence justified by his venerable deportment."[19] This "graceful demeanor" is hardly revealed in the Rembrandt portrait, perhaps because the subject is presented without gesture or any animation. A notable feature of this etching is its distinct artistry, the delicate lighting that falls on the dark hat, the black color being repeated upon the narrow scarf, which may indeed be meant to represent a praying-shawl, or *tallit*.[20]

Here, also, as in the etching of Ephraim Bonus, we are in possession of another graphic representation of this subject. The work in this instance is that of a Jewish artist, one Salom d'Italia, who had come to Holland from Italy (fig. 13). In contrast with this rather stilted engraving, the masterly treatment of Rembrandt's work is revealed with special intensity. In regarding this etching we can readily understand why the Jews, who desired their portraits

51

13. Salom d'Italia, "Manasseh ben Israel." Engraving.

painted or etched, turned, in most instances, to Christian artists.
The work of the Jewish painters and engravers of the time was of

52

a definitely inferior quality. Such artists as a Liebermann, a Josephson or an Epstein — to name three outstanding portraitists of our day — could only emerge in a period that brought to Jewish art an emancipation providing untrammelled liberty of expression.

With the exception of the portraits of Ephraim Bonus and Manasseh ben Israel we are unable to identify with absolute certainty any Jewish portraits of Rembrandt's. Attempts to this purpose have been made at various times. A portrait in the Uffizi Gallery in Florence, representing an old man seated at a table, is said to be that of Saul Levy Morteira, Chief Rabbi of the Amsterdam Portuguese Congregation from 1616 to 1660.[21] Evidence to this effect is suggested by a drawing to which we have referred in another connection, the scene of a circumcision, the work of a Dutch artist (fig. 3). The bearded man who towers above the hat of the godfather, shown *en face*, is supposed to be this Saul Levy Morteira, and his head to resemble that in the Uffizi picture. This assumption, however, is without basis, inasmuch as the drawing was made as late as 1665, and Morteira had died in 1660. If this evidence be disregarded, the contention falls into pure conjecture. We may, in fact, entertain a doubt as to the head in this painting being that of a Jew. The face with its straight nose might as readily be that of a Christian scholar.

Another investigator has claimed to have discovered the face of Baruch Spinoza in the painting "Man with a Magnifying Glass," now in the New York Metropolitan Museum.[22] As is well known, Spinoza earned his livelihood by polishing lenses. This portrait has, however, a companion-piece depicting a woman holding a car-

53

nation in her hand, indicating that the supposed Spinoza picture is that of a married man, while Spinoza remained a bachelor all his life. This assumption is, therefore, also without foundation, quite apart from the fact that the features of the man in this painting bear no resemblance to the well-authenticized portraits of Spinoza. Only recently, too, it has been declared, upon much better grounds, to be the portrait of the Dutch silversmith, Jan Lutma, the younger.[23] A silversmith, too, has use for a magnifying glass.

Attempts have more recently been made to identify the individuals shown in one of the most beautiful paintings of Rembrandt's later period, "The Jewish Bride," which hangs in the Rijkmuseum in Amsterdam (fig. 14). The picture depicts a man who, with a loving and infinitely tender gesture, touches a young woman. In this couple, a critic has claimed to have discovered the Sephardi poet Miguel de Barrios (1625–1701) and his second wife, the wealthy Abigail de Pina.[24] As evidence of the identification an engraving was produced showing this poet with his wife and his two children. We shall reproduce the picture for our readers, to afford them an opportunity of arriving at their own conclusion in the matter (fig. 15). A slight resemblance will, doubtless, be discerned between Abigail and the Jewish bride of the painting. The features are, however, too typical to invite a conclusive judgment. De Barrios, himself, reveals characteristic features in the engraving, a drawn-down mouth, an unattractive nose, a tense and troubled expression, befitting the highly nervous nature of this poet. The man in the Rembrandt painting, however, has a straight mouth and a strikingly well-modeled nose. His expression, too, is in no wise troubled or nervous, but is shown as calm and solemn.

The exalted dignity that emanates from the scene here depicted has led many an expert to the conclusion that no actual portraits are presented, but that Rembrandt is showing a pair of biblical lovers, Ruth and Boaz; or the young Tobias and his wife, Sarah; or Isaac and Rebekah. The face of the woman, however, would indicate that there is here a piece of portraiture. Her dress, her jewels and her entire presence reveal a definite and uncommon personality. The attire of the man, too, with the full, flowing, richly patterned sleeves, is not unusual in portraits of the period. The designation of the picture as "The Jewish Bride" was not established until some time in the 19th century. It would be possible to discern a Jewish type in the woman; but the slender, regular features of the man could not readily be associated with Jewish characteristics.[25] For these reasons the meaning of this painting must remain a mystery.

In several of Rembrandt's portraits there are some indications that hint at the probable vocations or professions of the sitters. There is a portrait of a man, in the National Gallery of London (fig. 16), which is generally believed to be that of a Jewish merchant, and this assumption is doubtless well founded. The features of the subject reveal characteristics of energy, if not stubbornness. The manner in which the hand grasps the handle of the cane suggests a grim determination to hold fast to the gains the man has acquired. The garments are of decided elegance; the fur cap is adorned with a bright feather; and the gray and white doublet, its sleeve resem-

14.   Rembrandt, "The Jewish Bride."   Painting.

15. Aaron de Chaves, "The Poet Miguel de Barrios and his Family." Drawing.
Engraving by Ch. v. Hagen.

16. Rembrandt, "Portrait of a Jewish Merchant." Painting.

bling that shown in the dress of the man in "The Jewish Bride," is fashioned of lustrous silk.

The impression created upon the beholder of Rembrandt's Jewish portraits is, in most cases, that of viewing personalities of spiritual eminence, men of scholarly inclination rather than those engaged in business. A number of these figures have throughout the years been designated as Rabbis. This opinion is strengthened by the fact that portraits of Rabbis were held in special affection by Jews, at any rate among those of Western Europe. There existed among them no princes or military chieftains to command their veneration, and, in consequence, their admiration was concentrated upon their spiritual leaders. Such portraits were frequently executed during the lifetime of these beloved Rabbis and graphic reproductions were widely distributed after their death, in order to keep alive their beneficent and benignant influence. It is very probable that Rembrandt fashioned several portraits of Rabbis, one of whom, Manasseh ben Israel, we have presented to our readers in these pages. The question that confronts us is whether *all* of the portraits classified as "Rabbis" are properly so designated. Their number is about fifteen, but there could not have been anything like so large a number of Rabbis in Amsterdam during the thirty or forty years of Rembrandt's residence in this city, even if we assume that an occasional Rabbi had come to Amsterdam as a visitor. There come into consideration, as we have shown, only the Sephardi Rabbis, and not any of either German or Polish origin. We are acquainted with the appearance of several of these through the work of other

59

17. Rembrandt, "An Old Jew at his Study Table." Painting.

artists: thus Isaac Aboab da Fonseca (1605–1693) and Jacob Sasportas (1610–1698).[26] These faces are not found in the work of Rembrandt, and consequently the number of possible rabbinical portraits from his brush is thereby still further restricted. It is, therefore, advisable to class the greater number of so-styled rabbinical portraits simply as pictures of Jews.

The Budapest Museum of Fine Arts possesses a painting, made in 1643, catalogued as that of a Rabbi (fig. 17). It is the portrait of an aged man wearing a heavy cloak over his doublet, the edge of which is embroidered in gold. Upon the table at his side there is shown a brass candlestick and a large book. That it is a Hebrew book is indicated by a slight circumstance: the volume is lying so that the cover would be raised toward the right, thus revealing the first page upon being opened. The inference that the book in the painting is a Hebrew, and at the same time a religious, work is strengthened by the fact that it reposes upon an ornate cushion, even as the scroll of the Torah in the synagogue is not permitted to touch the wood of the table on which it is placed, but must be protected by a handsome table cover. That it is a Jew who is here depicted admits of no doubt. But is the portrait that of a Rabbi? The garments of the old man bear no resemblance to the attire shown in the Manasseh ben Israel etching. The great age of the subject also militates against its being the portrait of any then officiating Rabbi. Besides this, a study of the Bible and the Talmud was part of the obligation resting upon every pious Jew.

Various other doubts are evoked in the consideration of this

61

painting. Was it in any sense intended as a specific portrait, or was it to be representative of a Jewish type? Rembrandt often painted pictures of Christian scholars, showing them engaged in writing, reading, or meditation, not to make a portrait, but merely because the theme in itself held an attraction for him. Why should he not, also, for the same reason have painted a Jewish scholar? In this instance he could himself have provided the costly garment, which the model may not have possessed, as Rembrandt is known to have been an assiduous collector of rare and beautiful textiles. Such pieces of wearing apparel, and other atelier properties, were utilized by the painter in various other paintings and served to lend an effective ensemble to his portrayals of scintillating Oriental scenes. The purchaser of such a painting would not have been, in any event, the individual selected for portrayal, but any art lover, Jewish or Christian, desirous of possessing the picture of an aged Jewish scholar, painted with the dignity, the artistry and the splendor of which Rembrandt's brush was capable.

It may have been with similar intention that a painting was executed by this artist a few years earlier, in 1635 (fig. 18). In this work there is presented an individual whose cloak, thrown over an embroidered doublet, is held together with a splendid golden clasp, and whose headgear is a jewelled turban. On the table in the background of the painting a slanted book is shown, while a serpent twines around a column. We are at once reminded of the brazen serpent that Moses ordered erected in the wilderness, so that those who had been bitten by serpents might find healing in looking upon it. The inclusion of this emblem in the painting has inclined some critics to the view that a biblical figure is here designed, either Moses or his brother, Aaron. But in all the representations of the High Priest known to me there is a breastplate studded with the twelve precious stones that symbolize the tribes of Israel. Earlier expounders have maintained that this portrait represented a Rabbi; but further consideration will lead to the same conclusion arrived at in the case of the old man shown in the Budapest painting. There was no Sephardi Rabbi of such age in the Amsterdam of 1635, nor any who could have worn a turban. The officiating Rabbis of that period had come to Amsterdam directly from the Iberian Peninsula, and had, without doubt, adopted the garb of their environment, as we have seen in the portrait of Manasseh ben Israel. It is possible that Jews wearing turbans had been seen in Amsterdam; but, if so, they would have been visitors from Islamic countries. Moroccan Jews especially maintained active commercial relations with their Amsterdam coreligionists.[27]

It seems probable to us that Rembrandt, although he had selected a definite model for his painting, had given it freest treatment. One of Rembrandt's earliest biographers cited the fact that the painter "could spend a day or two in adorning a turban in accordance with his own fancy."[28] It may be inferred that in this painting, too, he utilized some of his own material to construct the required turban. The costly and ornate breastplate may also have belonged to him and not to his model. The painting in its entirety depicts an Oriental, or more exactly, as the inclusion of the serpent would

18. Rembrandt, "An Oriental Jew." Painting.

19.   Rembrandt, "Portrait of a Jew."   Painting.

suggest, an Oriental Jew. As in the Budapest picture, there was no intention here of creating a portrait, but of making a picture of general interest designed for a general public. Many subsequent engravings of this work give evidence of the favor with which it was received, and this, too, would warrant the assumption that it gratified a general taste and was not intended to meet the wishes of an individual purchaser.

It is equally unlikely that the old man in a chair, painted in 1645 and now in the Berlin Museum (fig. 19), represents a Rabbi, although the dignity that emanates from this figure might well merit such a conclusion. In this case, too, we are confronted with the difficulty of identifying a man of his advanced age with any of the officiating Rabbis of the time. That this is, however, an actual portrait appears to admit of little question. There is, here, an absence of the adornment that marks the previously examined paintings and places them in a special classification. Such a hat, such a garment and cloak, and such a chain actually constituted the attire worn by the Hollanders in those days, and we have indicated how closely the habiliments of the Jews resembled those of their Amsterdam neighbors. Painted ten years later than was the Oriental Jew with the turban, the portrait of the Dutch Jew of 1645 reveals the direction that the development of Rembrandt's art as a portrait painter had taken: a greater simplicity in the means employed. Here the body and head are turned in the same direction and both are presented in full-front to the beholder. Despite this treatment, there is no monotony here, due to the difference in the hands and the play of light and shade on the features. A light is thrown on the right cheek, and the left is shaded; while a shadow, made by the brim of the hat, is spread over the eyes and the forehead. This effect of shadow lends an aspect of mildness and meditation to the face.

About ten years later in his career he made two paintings that represent the peak of Rembrandt's Jewish portrayals. One is that of the old Jew seated in an armchair, now in the Hermitage at Leningrad (fig. 20). In contrast to the upright-sitting Jew of the Berlin gallery, the pose here has a striking relevance; and one feels that this is how an aged man would be seated in his chair, with back slightly bent and the head bowed. Here is found the wearied, faded glance of the eyes of a very old person. His face is weather-worn with years, and many vicissitudes have graven deep furrows in his countenance.

The year 1654 witnessed the painting of the other of these portraits, likewise included in the Leningrad Hermitage collection (fig. 21). This is another painting of an old Jew, and he, too, is inclined to sit with folded hands. But Rembrandt did not repeat himself. In this work his model wears a broad-brimmed cap, and only the head faces the beholder, while the body and the chair are turned slightly toward the side. The double-pointed beard is somewhat more dishevelled than the neatly rounded one in the other portrait, and the features show a more uncouth and primitive expression with their large eyes and the prominent and energetic nose.

It may be that Rembrandt had the thought, when he beheld this old Jew, that the Jews were surely a remarkable people. Pursued

67

20.   Rembrandt, "Portrait of an Old Jew."   Painting.

21.   Rembrandt, "Portrait of an Old Jew."   Painting.

by misfortune throughout the ages, harassed, driven from their homes, tortured and burnt at the stake, they kept continually surviving, adapting themselves to the changing conditions of the times and countries, yet always remaining Jews in appearance and in their unswerving loyalty to their faith. Their features developed a somewhat sad and tired expression, combined with strong and uncompromising traits, as though they had been commanded by a higher power to remain steadfast until that distant day when a divine justice would be the portion of even the oppressed in this world.

We know but little concerning Rembrandt's portraits of Jewish women. That they had not proven of entirely negligible value may be gleaned from the previously mentioned incident of the commission given Rembrandt by Diego d'Andrada for the portrait of a young woman. Doubtless among many orders for the painting of Jewish men, companion pieces of their wives would be included. Such pictures of married couples are often found in the works of Rembrandt and in that of his contemporaries. Why should not the Jews, who held their women folk in such high esteem, have been similarly desirous of procuring their portraits? As with the men painted by Rembrandt, efforts have been made to identify the personality of one or another of these female portraits. Thus it has been assumed that the original of the lady shown holding a lap-dog (fig. 22) was the wealthy Abigail de Pina,[29] wife of the poet de Barrios, who, together with the members of his family, is portrayed in the engraving reproduced above (fig. 15). This may well be so. It is prob-

70

22.   Rembrandt, "Portrait of a Jewish (?) Lady."   Painting.

able that this lady, with her curved nose, was a Jewess, and her strikingly rich and elaborate costume could readily have been that of a member of the Jewish world of *haute finance*. For this reason we have included the picture in our collection, since the young Jewish women who sat to Rembrandt for their portraits may have resembled this figure.

We present here only a selection from the works of the artist, but they will suffice to establish the fact that Rembrandt's output of Jewish portraits formed a substantial part of the painter's productivity. Distinguished as works of art, they are, at the same time, representations of Jews, and provide us not only with a portrayal of their outward appearance but reveal in full measure their spiritual qualities. The Jewish fate, insofar as facial expression has ever mirrored it, has never been represented with such authenticity and such grandeur as in Rembrandt's Jewish portraits.

III

REMBRANDT'S SCENES OF JEWISH DAILY LIFE

WE HAVE indicated in the foregoing that various representations of Jewish men and women cannot in any accurate sense be designated as portraits. They had not been commissioned by individuals nor designed to be turned over to those who had posed to the artist, but had been the product of Rembrandt's artistic impulses and intended for the delectation of a coterie of art lovers. It appears strange to us that there should have been such a group, at any rate among Christians. Today one would look for them in vain. But they evidently existed in the Holland of the 17th century and manifested a lively interest, not only in the representation of individual Jews, but in the portrayal of scenes of Jewish daily life. For these art lovers Rembrandt had etched several plates, and the large number of impressions made from them indicates that the circle whom such works attracted could not have been a small one.

We must, to be sure, ask ourselves, in considering each one of these productions, whether the subject is actually based upon a Jewish theme, or whether such a designation was affixed to the work at a later date when the intimate relations that had existed between Rembrandt and the Jewish world of his day became better known.

A small etching of Rembrandt's exists, which, fashioned in 1639, has been entitled, as far back as the 18th century, "The Jew with the High Cap." It shows a poorly clad man, supporting himself on a cane which he holds in his right hand. Itinerant folk of this kind were frequently used as models by Rembrandt, and one such specimen of lowly life, "The Rat Killer," shown in an etching, resembles the above-mentioned Jew with the cap as one brother might another, and is surely not intended to represent a Jew. We must, therefore, hesitate to accept the Jewish designation of the latter picture, especially as this etching holds no suggestion of anything Jewish that would invite our interest in connection with this study.

There is, without doubt, equally little reason to include in our group of Jewish pictures the Rembrandt etching executed in the previous year and, in the past, generally designated "The Little Jewish Bride." This is a half-figure of a young woman with flowing tresses. On one side of the picture the section of a wheel has been discovered, the emblem of St. Catherine of Alexandria, who, as a martyr of the early Christian era, had been placed by her persecutors upon a spiked wheel, which had been miraculously shattered at the moment she was attached to it. Inasmuch as she was of royal descent, she is shown in this etching with a circlet on her head.

There exists, in addition to the etching of "The Little Jewish Bride," one styled "The Great Jewish Bride," so designated because of its considerably larger format (fig. 24). This, too, depicts a young woman with flowing hair, adorned with a circlet. She is splendidly attired and is shown seated in a chair holding a scroll in her hand,

74

while a number of books are displayed in the background of the room. This picture, too, has been robbed of its original title by modern experts who have pronounced it as representing Minerva, Goddess of Arts and Sciences (thus accounting for the books), or a Sibyl, the scroll in whose hand contains prophetic words.[30] In other instances, these elucidators added, Rembrandt had utilized the effect of flowing hair in his pictures to suggest legendary or mythological figures. This may be a correct deduction, but it would not affect the propriety of a similar treatment in depicting a Jewish bride. In contemporary writings it is specifically recorded that the Jewish bride arranged her hair in this fashion on the day of her wedding and, thus arrayed, would be escorted in ceremonial bridal procession to the home of the bridegroom. Ensconced in a special chair, she would be provided with beautiful garments and adorned with the bridal veil.[31] The bridal veil has not been forgotten in the etching. Attached to the back of the head, the veil first becomes visible in the picture under the left arm, drooping in narrow folds over the side of the chair. The circlet which adorns the head — a royal symbol — is at the same time a distinctive attribute of the Jewish bride, being a traditional ornament in this ceremonial. The bride appears on her wedding day wearing such a crown or circlet. The books shown in the background possess no ritual significance, but their appearance in a Jewish home would be most appropriate. The written scroll in the hand of the bride, however, is explainable on the basis of Jewish custom, which provided that the bride be presented with a written manifest (known as *ketubah*) containing

23.   Rembrandt, "The Jewish Bride."   Drawing.

24. Rembrandt, "The Jewish Bride." Etching.

a detailed schedule of the bridegroom's pledges for her maintenance, a description of what she would receive in the event of his death or of a justifiable separation. This custom harks back to Jewish antiquity, when the writings were in the form of inscriptions upon parchment, and these were preserved in the shape of scrolls. In keeping with their conservative character, the Jews have continued the use of these forms and scrolls, in the same manner as they have preserved both of them in the Torah. The pictured scroll in this etching is not bulky, but is exactly the size of the customary *ketubah*.

Rembrandt must have had frequent opportunities of seeing a Jewish bride, since he resided in the quarter of the city in which many Jews had their homes. In this instance his eyes had captured an impression (fig. 23) which took in the entire subject, rather than its details. For this reason the figure of the woman is presented completely while the features of the face are merely suggested. The etching was then developed from the hasty sketch of his pen; the garments carefully delineated with a wealth of light and dark contrasts. Observe the softly flowing hair of the girl and the heavy folds in the lower part of her gown. Only then did the artist proceed to the completion of the young woman's features. It is not a beautiful face, and is in no way designed to represent a saint or a goddess. But it is the true presentation of a face that Rembrandt took from its Jewish environment. He has here fashioned a genre-work and it may be assumed that purchasers of such etchings could have been Christians as well as Jews.

Another etching of Rembrandt's that affords an insight into the

78

25.   Rembrandt, "The Synagogue."   Etching.

daily life of the Jews is "The Synagogue," executed in 1648 (fig. 25).
A large interior is shown with the foreground brightly lighted, while
the background is in heavy shadow. At the extreme left are two old
men, one of small stature who stands erect, and a taller man who
is stooping so that the other may hear the better what he is saying.
At the right, two men, lost in thought, are shown walking toward
the front; two others are moving toward the rear; while between
them the back of another, who is seated, is drawn. There is, finally,
at the back of the picture, a group of three men. One wonders
whether the resulting total of ten figures in this picture is accidental
or intended, as it is well known that the presence of ten men (a
minyan) is necessary for a Jewish religious service.[32]

79

In this case, too, efforts have been made to give a different interpretation to the purpose of the artist. It is the contention of some that the structure is not a synagogue, but depicts the Temple of Jerusalem, and that the seated man is Judas stricken with remorse at his betrayal of Jesus.[33] Rembrandt had, it is known, utilized the Judas theme in the picture described above of "Judas Returning the Thirty Pieces of Silver" (fig. 4). We pointed out the dramatic manner in which the painter had given expression to the intensely moving episode; but he must have lost this gift of pictorial narration if we are to assume that the picture of the man shown with his back to the beholder is the remorseful Judas. This man is given a quite placid pose, and no one appears to notice his presence in either a friendly or inimical manner. This is not the Temple of Jerusalem — such an interpretation is clearly without basis — but the interior of a synagogue, and the figures are not personages in a historic episode, but representatives of everyday life.

Other questions inject themselves in the contemplation of this etching; for instance, what synagogue is here shown and what type of Jews are assembled within its walls? The Sephardi Jews, soon after their arrival in Amsterdam, had established three houses of worship, in part by reason of their rapidly increasing numbers, and in a measure due to ritualistic differences which, as is readily understandable, arose among groups just returned to their Jewish mode of life after having been posing as Christians. They had finally adjusted their disagreements and organized themselves into one congregation (*Talmud Torah*), reconstructing one of their synagogues,

26.   Romeyn de Hooghe "The Sephardic Synagogue in Amsterdam."   Engraving.

in the year 1639, into a stately edifice. This building is no longer in existence, and vanished from memory after the erection, in 1675, of the large Portuguese synagogue which is still standing. We are, however, in possession of engravings which show the exterior and interior of the old synagogue. The outside (fig. 26) has the appearance of a two-storied palace, with high pilasters between its windows. The interior (fig. 27) shows an extensive hall, divided by columns into three sections, a broad nave in the center and two narrower aisles at the sides. The columns support galleries for the women worshippers.

Nothing here described is to be seen in Rembrandt's "The Synagogue." The picture shows one undivided room, without either columns or galleries.

An examination of the attire of the visitors to the synagogue of 1639, shown in figure 27, again reveals these Amsterdam Sephardim as wearing the customary broad-brimmed hats, the white collars and the short cloaks of their environment. In contrast to this apparel, the Jews in Rembrandt's etching are garbed in cloaks that reach to the ground, and hats of which several tower high on their heads. This may have been the habit worn by the Ashkenazi Jews who had dwelt in their ghettos for centuries, segregated from Christian populations, and who had not changed the fashion of their garments even after they had come to reside in Holland.

The interior of Rembrandt's synagogue seems also to indicate its Ashkenazi character. The German Jews, who had at first participated in the Sephardi mode of worship, later detached themselves in order

82

27. I. Veenhuysen, "Interior of the Sephardic Synagogue in Amsterdam." Engraving.

to practice their own ritual, which differed from that of the Sephardim. Already in 1635 they conducted services in a room of their own, which they exchanged in 1639 for larger quarters; and in 1646 plans were considered for the erection of a house of worship of their own. We have no positive knowledge as to whether these plans were ever carried out, as the Hollanders placed many hindrances in their way. Neither do we know what these various places of worship looked like, since no description or portrayal has come down to us. We must take for granted that they were less ornate than those of the Sephardim, in consequence of the more limited resources at their disposal in those days. They could have had no columns nor galleries for their women-folk, who, according to German usage, sat in wings constructed for their separate accommodation and connected with the main chamber, if at all, only by openings in these extensions.[34]

The door in these Ashkenazi synagogues was often placed at one side, as though the entrance was to be as inconspicuous as possible. Several steps usually led from the portal down to the ground floor. This construction was founded upon the well-known words of the 130th Psalm: "Out of the depths have I called to Thee, O Lord!" a phrase that already in the Talmud (B. Ta'anit 23b) had been interpreted literally, and in accordance with which the ground floor of the synagogue was generally placed at a lower level than the portal. Rembrandt in his etching over-emphasized this detail of the steps, evidently as a result of the profound impression made upon him by the symbolism implied in this humility toward God.

From this point of view Rembrandt's "Synagogue" has an important historical significance. It furnishes us with a picture of the German Jews of the middle of the 17th century, and of the houses in which they assembled for worship. We must, however, bear in mind that Rembrandt was not an architectural designer in the customary sense of the word. He may have, at times, made architectural drawings as such, and then he reproduced every building faithfully. Where, however, he introduced such a building in an etching or in a painting, he was content to subordinate its importance in order not to detract from the interest he desired to evoke in the human figures of his portrayals.

Rembrandt was not the first Christian artist to depict a synagogue. One hundred and thirty years before his etching, a German, Albrecht Altdorfer, made one of the interior of the Regensburg synagogue, following this with a similar plate showing the vestibule of this structure (fig. 28). This vestibule, it appears, served as a prayer room for women. The floor of the main synagogue hall, in which the men of the congregation assembled for worship, was on a lower level, as may be inferred from the bent knee of the man stepping into the hall. The impulse to the creating of these etchings was the destruction of the synagogue in the year 1519, during an attack by a frenzied mob which had been goaded to fury against the Jews whom they then drove from the city. Latin inscriptions on small tablets at the top of both etchings record these disastrous happenings. The inscription on the vestibule plate reads: "The Vestibule of the Synagogue of the Jews of Ratisbon, destroyed on the 21st day of February, in the year 1519." The other tablet reads: "In the year of our Lord, 1519, the Ratisbon Jewish Synagogue, by the righteous judgment of God, was utterly demolished." The German artist's interest in this synagogue is thus shown to derive from his satisfaction at its destruction.

Could there be any better illustration of the general attitude toward the Jews of Germany in the 16th century than that provided by these two etchings of the Regensburg synagogue? And could there be a more vivid contrast to this condition than is revealed by Rembrandt's work as existing in the Holland of the 17th century? Here, for the first time in Europe, the Jews, who had been unwillingly tolerated and in continual danger of expulsion, were enabled to live in safety and were regarded with interest by the best elements of the community.

A few years prior to the creation of the Rembrandt etching, Queen Henrietta Maria of England had paid a visit to the imposing Sephardi synagogue of Amsterdam (though not to the Ashkenazi house of worship). This was in 1642, when she came to this city to present her ten-year-old daughter to her youthful bridegroom, the son of Holland's Stadtholder. On this occasion the Sephardi community received the Queen with elaborate ceremonial, and Manasseh ben Israel preached a specially prepared sermon in honor of the illustrious guest.

Due to his wide scholarship, his elegant diction, and his lovable and kindly personality, this Rabbi had won the esteem, not only of the Jews, but of the Christian elements of the community. Proudly he could say of himself, in one of his writings: "I have enjoyed the friendship of the wisest and most illustrious men of Europe."[35] It

28. Albrecht Altdorfer, "The Synagogue of Ratisbon." Etchings.

was this Manasseh ben Israel whom Rembrandt immortalized in his celebrated portrait of the great Rabbi, who, as we shall learn, approached Rembrandt with the request that he provide illustrations for one of his books. The artist was willing to comply with his wish. He was evidently aligned with that section of the community which desired to promote a better understanding between the Jews and Christians. With this urge he painted Jewish faces, not only for those who had ordered them as portraits, but as a champion of the Jewish people; and he apparently found purchasers for such pictures among non-Jews. The same impulse led to his etchings of "The Jewish Bride" and "The Synagogue;" the artist's purpose, in these creations, far from being anti-Jewish, was the promoting of an unprejudiced interest in Jewish customs.

His attitude in this matter found imitators. Several years after the appearance of the synagogue etching, the Dutch painter, Jacob Ruisdael, visited the Sephardi burial ground in Ouderkerk, near Amsterdam, and made two drawings of its oldest tombstones, having been attracted by their unusual design. Prints of these drawings were made by the artists Abraham Bloteling and Romeyn de Hooghe. Before the publication of these prints, Jacob Ruisdael utilized his tombstone drawings as the main feature of a work of art that has been accorded world-wide fame. This is the painting of "The Jewish Cemetery," in the Dresden Museum, in which these stones, together with a mouldering ruin, a decayed tree, a raging torrent and storm-driven clouds combine to produce an effect of romantic melancholy (fig. 29).[36]

88

29. Jacob Ruisdael, "The Jewish Cemetery." Painting.

It was thus that Jewish themes found expression in the development of the Christian art of that period and won European recognition. It redounds to the credit of Rembrandt that, due to his initiative, a new and important vista was opened to the creative art of the world.

IV

REMBRANDT AND THE BIBLE

THE Jewish theme! In one sense it had long been known to Christian art — in scenes of biblical life; in pictures of Old Testament stories. The Jewish injunction against graven images had cast its prohibitive shadow also upon early Christian art, and many had raised the question whether it were permissible to make a representation of anything "that is in heaven above, or that is in the earth beneath, or that is in the water under the earth." We now know that Jewish art, too, had given, in the early days of the Christian era, a more liberal interpretation to the restrictions contained in the Second Commandment than had formerly been supposed. In a Syrian synagogue of the third century of our era, in Dura-Europos, archeologists have uncovered the ruins of a synagogue the walls of which from the floor to the ceiling were covered with scenes of the biblical story.[37] The principle that governed these portrayals was based upon the interpretation that the Second Commandment did not prohibit the representation of objects, but their worship. The emphasis was on "Thou shalt not bow down to them nor serve them." And besides, it was more difficult for the Christian religion to forego the use of representative art than it was for the Jewish.

91

The followers of the latter had learned to read already in their childhood, and were in consequence capable at all times of visualizing in their spirit the incidents of Bible history. Christianity, on the contrary, had made its inroads largely among illiterate peoples or, at any rate, among illiterate classes of the communities. To them the pictorial representation served as a means of instruction, or, as Pope Gregory the Great expressed it: "The picture takes the place of the reading for the population. They read at least upon the walls what they are unable to read in books."

This Christian art placed scenes of the Old Testament in a natural and harmonious association with scenes from the New Testament and the lives of the saints. Both worlds, the Jewish and the Christian, were not opposed, but were intimately related in the Christian mind: the Old Testament formed the threshold of the promise; the New Testament its fulfillment. What lies hidden, in the first, steps into the light in the second. For this reason the Middle Ages never ceased to represent the Old Testament incidents, for these served to fortify the Christian faith, to the portrayal of which the entire art of the Middle Ages was dedicated.

The Renaissance, that followed upon the Middle Ages, continued these biblical portrayals with undiminished ardor. While the representation of historical and mythical phases of Antiquity achieved a wide popularity, there was no relaxation in the artistic treatment of themes of biblical significance, inasmuch as the Christian faith retained its intensity. On the contrary, the Renaissance provided many new aspects of Bible art. The beauty-cult of this period was embodied in pictures of the young and gentle Tobias or in the sculptured nudity of David. Its pleasure in the representation of physical grandeur was expressed in the approval bestowed upon such figures as Moses or the valiant-hearted Judith. Michelangelo even endeavored, in those incomparably beautiful frescoes of the Sistine Chapel, to depict his conception of the creative power of the Almighty in the scenes showing the creation of the world and of man made in God's image.

Protestantism interrupted the progress of this trend for a brief period. The fear of idol-worship brought about a reaction against the inclusion of figures from the Bible and from the story of saints in the churches and chapels of the new creed. At the same time the realm of art was extended to include new provinces. Portraiture had already been added to its domain in the years of the Renaissance, and now it directed its interest to phases of landscape painting, the portrayal of scenes from daily life, objects of still-life, and the like.

But the creation of biblical pictures had not by any means been discontinued. This phase of art still flourished in all the Catholic countries: in Italy, in France, in Spain, in Belgium, and even in the Protestant lands of Northern Europe, including the little country of Holland. This fact must be especially emphasized, inasmuch as an American critic, John C. van Dyke, has advanced a peculiar theory regarding Rembrandt's biblical pictures.[38] He simply denies the Rembrandt authorship of most of them, and attributes their origin freehandedly to his pupils. He bases his contention upon the fact that the Calvinist movement had placed a ban upon the presence

93

of biblical pictures in the churches of Holland, and that the above-mentioned newer themes had been given prominence in the homes of the Dutch people. A few of those biblical paintings, which this critic admits to have been the work of Rembrandt, are maintained by him not to have been executed upon commissions, nor to have been the product of any inner urge on the part of the artist, but to have been designed for the instruction of his many pupils, who later on continuously made use of what they had learned from their master.

It is truly astonishing to think that Rembrandt should have based his instruction upon examples of art which would never find purchasers. But setting aside this peculiar contention, van Dyke is mistaken as to the attitude adopted by the Hollanders in the matter of biblical pictures. The Calvinists, doubtless, excluded biblical scenes from their places of worship, and filled their private homes with portraits, landscapes and genre-pictures. Nevertheless, paintings of sacred themes also found places upon their walls. In one of Rembrandt's etchings, "The Gold-Weigher," a wall is adorned with a picture of "The Brazen Serpent," from the well-known story about Moses. In like manner, scenes of biblical import continued to be part of the embellishment of the town halls and guild halls throughout the land.

It should further be borne in mind that the population of Holland included, besides the Protestants, a by no means inconsiderable number of Catholics, who did decorate their places of worship, if not ostentatiously on the exteriors, still within the walls, with scenes of biblical stories, and surely would have felt no hesitation in placing orders for paintings with Protestant artists when those of their own faith were not available. Many of Rembrandt's paintings, whose subjects are foreign to Protestant ideology, doubtless originated in this manner.

A final argument in this connection may be based on the fact that purchasers of pictures depicting biblical themes included members of the new Jewish community, at least its Sephardi element. We have indicated in the foregoing that the latter placed a more liberal interpretation upon the ban against pictorial representations than had their forebears in the Middle Ages, or their contemporary Ashkenazi coreligionists. This led to their interest in and acceptance of portraiture. And now they went even a step farther, and admitted biblical pictures to their homes, though they did not permit them in their synagogues. We have shown, in a drawing made in 1665 by a Dutch artist (fig. 3), the interior of a room in the home of a wealthy member of the Jewish community. On the wall at the back hang two pictures, the lower part of one being clearly visible, while the greater part of the other is hidden behind a canopied four-poster bed. Although the subject of the latter picture is not recognizable, the former depicts the kneeling figure of a bearded man in a state of intense agitation, with outspread arms. An angel with arm extended is shown in the air, addressing the kneeling man. This is the angel who brings to Moses, at the Burning Bush, the revelation of his mission. The pathetic style of this painting has no bearing upon Rembrandt's work, but we may assume from its presence in this home that the Jews had not only given commissions to Rembrandt for portraits but had also purchased from him pictures based upon biblical themes.

In one instance these pictures were not paintings, but etchings intended for use as illustrations for a printed text, the author of which was the Rabbi Manasseh ben Israel, to whom frequent reference has been made in these pages. The title of this book was *Piedra Gloriosa; o, De la Estatua de Nebuchadnesar* (The Glorious Stone, or Nebuchadnezzar's Statue). Manasseh ben Israel wrote this book in 1654 or 1655, and it was published in a very small format, $2\frac{7}{8}$ x $5\frac{1}{2}$ inches, a miniature size much in favor at that time. The Rabbi shared the belief, entertained by many Jews of his day, that the Messiah would shortly make his appearance. He found evidence for this expectation in the dream of the Babylonian King Nebuchadnezzar, as related in the second chapter of the Book of Daniel. In this dream the king had beheld a statue, the head wrought of fine gold, the breast and arms of silver, the belly and loins of brass, the legs of iron, the feet in part of iron and in part of clay. Suddenly a stone detached itself, smiting the statue's feet, which were destroyed together with the entire image. This stone became a great mountain and filled the whole earth.

Daniel interpreted the king's dream by saying that the stone represented the Messianic Kingdom of God which would destroy all the kingdoms of the earth. This very stone, asserts Manasseh ben Israel in his work, served as the resting place of Jacob when there came to him the dream of the angels ascending and descending the ladder that extended between earth and heaven. It was also the

30. Rembrandt, "Jacob's Ladder." Etching.

same stone, he contended, that had later been hurled by David against Goliath. All this is comprehended in Daniel's vision of the four strange beasts and the Messiah, who stands in prayer before the Throne of God, surrounded by the heavenly hosts.

To provide illustrations for this elaborately fantastic dissertation, which had its inception in the ever-present yearning of the Jew for the Kingdom of God, Manasseh solicited Rembrandt's co-operation,

97

which the artist readily accorded. He made four etchings: the statue seen by Nebuchadnezzar; Jacob's dream of the ladder of the angels; the slaying of Goliath by David, and the Messianic Vision of Daniel (not the Vision of Ezekiel, as has often been asserted in this connection).

Rembrandt must have experienced some difficulties in meeting Manasseh's requirements, as repeated revisions were made in the plates. The statue of Nebuchadnezzar's dream, for instance, exists in five different forms, the last of which bears inscriptions on various parts of the figure, indicating the kingdoms destroyed by the Divine Will.[39] In the etching of Jacob's ladder (fig. 30) the figure of Jacob is not lying on the ground in the customary attitude, but is placed against the middle rung of the ladder, which symbolizes Jerusalem, the center of the world.

The simplest treatment is provided in the picture of the David-Goliath encounter, the contrast between the two men being graphically portrayed. The as-yet-undefeated giant is shown in full battle attire, while the small David is garbed in a loose jacket, armed with only his slingshot (fig. 31). In "The Vision of Daniel" (fig. 32), Rembrandt depicted an earthly zone with the four fantastic beasts, and the celestial realm containing the figures of the Messiah and kneeling angels, and God seated upon His throne, "His raiment white as snow."

When these etchings appeared in the Manasseh book, they must have shocked prospective purchasers. This would explain why so few copies of this edition are extant—one of them is in the library

98

31. Rembrandt, "David and Goliath." Etching.

of the Hebrew Union College in Cincinnati—and why other illustrations replaced Rembrandt's very soon thereafter. We do know that the Rembrandt plates were not accepted, and that other illustrations were used in their stead, either before publication of the book or after it had found its first purchasers. An unknown artist was commissioned, whose rather uncouth copper plates, as compared with the delicately wrought etchings of Rembrandt, introduced many changes in the treatment of the subjects.[40]

32.   Rembrandt, "The Vision of Daniel." Etching.

The most important of these, which we here present to our readers (fig. 33), is shown in the plate depicting the Vision of Daniel. In this the representation of God is effaced, and in its place the artist gives us an oval nimbus. It is probable that the main objection to Rembrandt's etching was to this picturing of the Almighty, inasmuch as it definitely violated the commandment "Thou shalt not make unto thee a graven image." While the Sephardi Jews of Amsterdam

33. Anonymous, "The Vision of Daniel."
Engraving.

might tolerate the presence of biblical scenes in pictures on the walls of their houses and biblical illustrations in their books, there was a limit to such portrayals beyond which they would not go.

Did Rembrandt take offense at the fact that his work failed to find approval? And were the friendly relations between him and Manasseh ben Israel, if such had existed, impaired by this happening? If so, the consequences are not apparent. In the same year that saw the publication of the *Piedra Gloriosa*, the illustrious Rabbi left Holland for England, to devote himself to the realization of his Messianic dream. It had been prophesied that this event would be preceded by a dispersal of the Jewish people to all parts of the world; and in the fulfillment of this purpose it was necessary that England, which had for centuries refused admission to the Jews, should now open its portals to them. In 1657 Manasseh returned to Holland gravely ill, and he died in the same year.

If we ask ourselves what Rembrandt's attitude was towards the presentation of biblical themes, regardless of any Jewish influences, we must recognize the fact that his relations to the Sacred Writings had been of the most intimate nature since the days of his early youth. It was a feature of Protestantism that it brought its followers into direct contact with the Bible, whereas the Catholic Church had been content to draw the teachings of Christianity from the Bible but had withheld the Sacred Book from the people owing to some objectionable passages. Then, too, it is certain that Rembrandt's mother had been a constant reader of the Bible. In various pictures Rembrandt depicted her with a large Bible on her lap, absorbed in the perusal of its pages (fig. 34). She, doubtless, instilled a deep piety in her children, and the imaginative Rembrandt must have listened with vivid interest as she read aloud the words of the Sacred Writings.

He retained this piety in his later years. At one time, when asked to inscribe a sentiment in an album, he wrote:

"Een vroom gemoet
Acht eer voor goet."

34. Rembrandt, "Rembrandt's Mother Reading the Bible." Painting.

"A pious mind prizes honor above worldly goods." In the conclud-ing words of letters of his which have been preserved, there are fre-quent turns of a pious nature.[41]

From the time his mother had read aloud to him from the big volume that contained both the Old and the New Testament, he had often looked into the Book himself and had gathered ever new inspiration from its pages. Both the Old and the New Testament provided subjects for his artistic output, and if one should, pedan-tically, make an inventory of his paintings, etchings and drawings, one may find a balance favoring New Testament themes. And yet the impression prevails that the Old Testament held a greater at-traction for him than the New. The latter may have exercised a more intense religious fascination upon him. The figure of Jesus undoubtedly touched his heart as an ideal, especially the Jesus who loved little children, the poor and the suffering, and who told the parable of the Prodigal Son, the story of the father whose affection for the repentant son was greater than his love for the righteous one.[42]

It was the Old Testament, however, that especially spurred his imagination. It contained not *one* outstanding figure, but many who were revealed in human activities and suffering; not as gods, but as mortals — mortals endowed with tremendous potentialities. Fried-rich Nietzsche, in his *Beyond Good and Evil*, gave the following telling expression of this experience: "In the Jewish Old Testament, the book of divine justice, there are men, things, and sayings on such an immense scale, that Greek and Indian literature have nothing

104

to compare with it. One stands with fear and reverence before those stupendous remains of what man was formerly, and one has sad thoughts about old Asia and its little out-pushed peninsula, Europe, which would like, by all means, to figure before Asia as the 'Progress of Mankind.' " Nietzsche, in his veneration for the Old Testament, goes so far as to subordinate the New Testament to it, and cannot understand how the Christians could have bound these two books into one volume as *the* Bible. Rembrandt, surely, did not go so far in his attitude to the subject, but he would have subscribed literally to Nietzsche's thought in his *Genealogy of Morals,* in which he said: "All honor to the Old Testament! I find therein great men, an heroic landscape, and one of the rarest phenomena in the world, the incomparable naïveté of the strong heart; further still, I find a people." Rembrandt may have regarded the Old Testament, in like manner, as a stage-setting of the world's great happenings, related with splendid ingenuousness.

The affection in which the Bible was held by Rembrandt was not peculiar to him in the Holland of the 17th century, but was shared by the entire population. The people of Holland, comparatively small in number, had thrown off the yoke of the powerful Spanish oppressor, as the children of Israel, also an oppressed group, had freed themselves from their Egyptian taskmasters. The Hollanders drew comparisons between their own destiny and that of the Jews, and looked upon themselves as a people similarly chosen by God, and, like the Jews, under His special providence. They admired the wisdom with which the Israelites, thanks to the leadership of Moses, had developed their communal life, and found therein a ground plan for the establishment of their own young Republic. In the year 1617, Professor Peter Cunaeus, a member of the faculty of the University of Leyden — the city in which Rembrandt had been born and reared — published a book entitled *De Republica Hebraeorum*, the preface of which opened with the words: "I offer to your view a commonwealth, the most holy and exemplary in all the world, because its author and founder was not a mortal man, but the immortal God, that God whose pure veneration and worship you have undertaken and which you maintain." This enables us to understand why the Town Hall of Amsterdam was adorned with a picture of Moses holding the tablets of the Law. The Hollanders saw in the Decalogue a bond of primal importance in their lives.

In the theaters of Holland, in those days, plays based on Old Testament themes were frequently presented. In 1618 Abraham de Koning's *The Tragedy of Samson* was published. Nicolaes Vonteyn's play, *Esther, or the Picture of Obedience*, appeared in the same year. Holland's foremost poet, Joost van den Vondel, wrote two dramas based upon incidents from the story of Joseph, and translated a third from the Latin of Hugo Grotius, the celebrated Dutch jurist. Two of these dramas were produced in 1640, and after 1653 all three of the plays were given repeatedly as a trilogy. It can admit of no doubt that in a time of such popularity for biblical drama, pictorial representations of themes of this nature should have been in demand, and that Rembrandt's work along the same lines found ready acceptance.

106

When we survey the entire output of biblical subjects in Rembrandt's paintings, etchings and drawings, we find that, while they include almost every phase of the Sacred Writings, there are certain themes that held a special attraction for him. The days of Creation, which Michelangelo had painted with such magnificent effect, are not represented in Rembrandt's work. His interest was not evoked by such cosmic happenings. What fascinated him in the omnipotence of the Almighty was only its manifestation in its relation to human beings. The Bible, to him, began with Adam and Eve; not with their creation, but with their transgression.

From this point he followed the main figures of Genesis: Cain and Abel, Noah, Abraham, Isaac and Jacob, and, finally, Joseph. The youth of the latter may have recalled to him the days of his own youth, when he stood out among his brothers, and cherished dreams of fame. In these portrayals he manifested as great an ardor for solemn and supra-natural happenings as for the human — all too human — incidents. He took much pleasure in introducing a representation of the Almighty, together with that of Abraham at the age of ninety-nine — related in Genesis 17.1: "And when Abraham was ninety years old and nine, the Lord appeared to Abraham . . ." and in picturing the verse of Genesis 18.1: "And the Lord appeared unto him by the terebinths of Mamre . . ." But he delighted equally in depicting the wanton daughters of Lot in their approach to their drunken father; and he achieved a remarkable success in the expression he has given the face of the befuddled, loud-singing man.

The story of Moses was subordinated in Rembrandt's work. He was not interested in great masses of people, preferring the play of individual relations in small groups. He painted the lovely scene of the rescue of the infant Moses from the Nile by the daughter of Pharaoh, and the giving of the Law on Sinai, but in the latter probably presented only Moses himself and not the multitude.

A single but powerful drawing was all that he gave as representative of the Book of Joshua. It shows the "captain of the hosts of the Lord" appearing with drawn sword before Joshua at Jericho.

His interest in the Book of Judges was especially directed to the story of Samson. The strength of this man, contrasted with his weakness in his attitude toward women, may have mirrored his own characteristics to the artist.

In the story of Saul he pictured in a striking manner the melancholy of the king. But here, too, he did not hesitate to make a daringly realistic drawing that showed Saul in the cave — "to cover his feet," as the Bible reads — being surprised by David, who secretly cut off the skirt of Saul's robe. This scene was given by Rembrandt without any restraint.

He comprehended David, as did the inspired narrator in the Bible, in all his aspects. This was the hero who already in his youth had slain Goliath; this is the eternal lover, who for the sake of a beautiful woman, Bathsheba, committed a serious sin; and this was the religiously inspired poet whose prayers were the Psalms that mount into the heavens.

The prophets were not envisaged by Rembrandt, as they had been by Michelangelo, as superhuman personalities, but as individuals like himself, to be presented as involved in human activities. The miraculous incidents of the Elijah and Elisha narratives were circumstantially portrayed. Rembrandt's Jeremiah is not represented, as is that of Michelangelo, merely in profound mourning over the destruction of the Temple, but also as engaged in a definite task. There seems to me no shadow of doubt that Rembrandt fell back upon II Maccabees, where it is related that the prophet hid the treasures of the Temple in a certain cave, there to rest until the day of redemption (II Maccabees 2.5–8). We place the Michelangelo mural alongside the panel of Rembrandt (figs. 35 and 36), and ask the reader to bear in mind our earlier analysis of the differences that marked the art of the Renaissance from that of the Baroque. Michelangelo unfolds to the beholder a clear and vivid picture of the prophet. Every detail is recognizable; the colors in their brightness emphasize the distinctness of the various parts of the body, and even the light and shade are utilized to clarify the portrayal. Rembrandt, on the other hand, presents his figure in sharp foreshortening, almost a third of the outline being obscured by a boulder in the foreground. The light is concentrated upon the bald head of the Prophet. At the base is shown the scintillating metal of a Temple ornament, while the other details of the picture are shadowed in the darkness of the cave.

Even before Rembrandt had been asked by Manasseh ben Israel to provide an etching for the already-mentioned Vision of Daniel, he

35. Michelangelo, "Jeremiah." Mural.

36. Rembrandt, "Jeremiah." Painting.

had painted another one of Daniel's visions, that of the strangely-horned ram. Rembrandt had on one occasion been afforded an opportunity of seeing some lions — a rare experience in those days — and had associated therewith the story of Daniel remaining unscathed in the den of wild beasts because of the constancy of his faith in God. That other story in the Book of Daniel, describing the feast of Belshazzar, at which the mysterious writing appeared upon the wall, was also an incentive to the brush of the artist.

His instinct for dramatic portrayal led Rembrandt to the Book of Esther, that story of grave peril to the Jewish people, as well as of their happy salvation. Here he found, at the same time, an opportunity of depicting royal splendor; and Rembrandt, the child of the people, was fascinated by everything bright and scintillating.

In the apocryphal books, omitted from the Hebrew Bible, but included in Rembrandt's Dutch volume of the Scriptures, he merely touched upon the Book of Judith, but was untiringly absorbed in the Book of Tobit. There was hardly a scene of this narrative, in itself a masterpiece of everyday naturalism, but became grist to the mill of Rembrandt's art. The old Tobit — and this forms the starting-point of the story — is here pictured at the moment in which he is blinded by the droppings of a sparrow.[43] The artist's interest in the narrative was especially directed to the scene in which the blind, suspicious old man loses faith in the unshakable honesty of his wife as she comes to him with a kid. The angel appears who accompanies the young Tobias on his travels, in which the latter experiences strange adventures, returning finally with a healing ointment for his father's blindness and with the woman he had chosen as a wife. Rembrandt portrays this healing scene with an accuracy of treatment as though depicting an operation for the removal of a cataract, excepting for the introduction of an angel with towering wings in the attitude of an assistant. After the completion of his beneficent work the angel departs in rapid flight, leaving the members of the family awed and amazed.

He was, finally, attracted to the story of Susannah — also included in the Apocrypha and, therefore, not a part of the Bible the Jews were accustomed to read — and he was prone to paint the incident of the maiden in her bath being spied upon by the two lustful old men. This subject was a popular one among artists since the period of the Renaissance, as it provided opportunity for the portrayal of beauty in the nude. Rembrandt was by no means averse from such portrayal in either his religious or mythological paintings. In the latter realm he gave us the undraped Danaë, as she received the golden shower of Zeus.[44] It would not have made much difference to him in such matters whether the theme were of biblical or of classical origin. We emphasize this contention in order to obviate any suggestion that Rembrandt may have created every one of his Bible pictures from impulses of piety. His approach to these subjects might be compared to that of the Sacred Writings themselves. The Bible is a religious work in the highest sense, but it occasionally provides "primrose paths of dalliance" without apparent purpose or restraint. And it is in this spirit that Rembrandt comprehended the Bible: as a sacred book, but also as a colorful, even in some places as a cheerful book, comparable to a world in which the great and the small, the exalted and the lowly dwell in harmonious association.

It was unnecessary for Rembrandt to invent the themes used by him in the majority of his biblical paintings; they were traditional in the realm of art. But he was in no wise content to produce slight variations of the work of other artists, and his individual touch endowed his Bible pictures with distinctive originality.

If we ask upon what principles these variations were based, we are again confronted, in quite a number of cases, with Jewish influences. Rembrandt was, in essence, a naturalist, aiming to approach nature as closely as possible. He now beheld from his windows Jews who were the descendants of those biblical figures that had so deeply interested him, and their presence suggested the idea of utilizing them in his paintings. The carrying out of this desire was made the more welcome to him by the fact that his own people, the Hollanders, possessed a placid, unemotional temperament, while the Jews were a people of quick sensibility and animation, easily stirred to joy or sorrow, and revealing these traits in the play of their features and in their gestures. These were the characteristics he sought for his creative work. Inasmuch as by the limitations of his art he was unable to reproduce the spoken words associated with action, he had to find a substitute in pantomimic expression, and was delighted to discover models that manifested their emotions not only in speech but in movement.

In some instances the changes made by Rembrandt in the characteristics provided by his models limited themselves to only slight

114

37. Rembrandt, "Jacob Caressing his Son Benjamin." Etching.

variations from the originals. He saw, for instance, an old man in
the act of fondling a child. The artist was attracted by a scene so
representative of the intimacy of Jewish family life. He placed an
apple in the hand of the lively youngster and proceeded to make
his drawing. He then provided a cushion for the seat of the chair,
placed a beautiful flower by its side, and the result was a biblical
etching: either Abraham caressing his son Isaac, or Jacob caressing Benjamin, his youngest son (fig. 37).

115

In another etching, Rembrandt has given us a picture from the Book of Esther — "The Triumph of Mordecai" (fig. 38). Mordecai, as a reward for having uncovered the plot against the life of the king, has been arrayed in royal robes and escorted through the streets of the city mounted on a magnificently apparelled horse, the while Haman, his adversary, is compelled to proclaim before him: "Thus shall it be done unto the man whom the king delighteth to honor." Here the king and Esther are shown sitting in a loge; the populace grouped about the beautifully caparisoned horse; but mounted upon this steed we see none other than the same aged Jew whom we remember from the Jacob and Benjamin etching. Upright he sits upon the horse, facing the beholder, but on his face there is a somewhat sceptical expression; for a Jew would have a realization of the rapidity with which the royal favor of today might be changed into hatred and persecution on the morrow or the day following.

Rembrandt went even a step beyond the Old Testament narratives in the matter of introducing the Jewish type in his paintings and etchings; it appears, also, in his New Testament portrayals. This had been done to some extent in earlier periods. In scenes depicting the life of Jesus there are shown, here and there, some typical Jewish figures; but they belonged to the persecutors, the betrayers of Jesus, not to his adherents. As a matter of course, Jesus usually is presented with an un-Jewish cast of features. His was an idealized face depicted by every people in accordance with its own conception of the beautiful and the noble. Rembrandt was the first artist courageous enough to show Jesus with Jewish features. It was evidently clear to him that

116

38.   Rembrandt, "The Triumph of Mordecai."   Etching.

Jesus was a Jew; as it had been to Martin Luther, more than a century earlier, *That Jesus Christ Was a Born Jew* — this being the actual title of a treatise published by Luther in 1523, at a time when he still cherished the hope that he might, with a friendly approach, induce the Jewish people to adopt the Christian faith — *his* form of Christian faith. "And though we take high pride in ourselves," he stated in this writing, "we are still heathens, and the Jews are of the race of Christ; we are but collateral kin and strangers, while they are blood relations, cousins and brothers of our Lord." Later, though, when the Jews resisted his efforts toward their conversion, Luther's attitude changed to one of hatred and persecution.

Hugo Grotius (1583–1645), the eminent Dutch jurist and statesman, who was a contemporary of Rembrandt's, gave expression to the same concept. He said: "We know very well that they (the Jews) are the offspring of holy men, whom God often visited by His prophets and His angels; that the Messiah was born of their nation, as were the first teachers of Christianity. They were the stock into which we were grafted."[45]

It is probable that Rembrandt had gleaned this viewpoint, if not from Luther's treatise, from the writing of his townsman. If Jesus was a Jew, he concluded, why should he not be pictorially represented as such? In our description of Rembrandt's Jewish portraits, we referred to his painting of the head of a young Jew (fig. 6), probably an Ashkenazi Jew, inasmuch as the features are not stamped with the pride of the Sephardim, but reveal the suffering that grew out of many centuries of persecution. The style of this work indicates its origin in the forties of the 17th century. It was in this period,

118

explicitly in 1648, that Rembrandt painted the picture of Jesus shown after the resurrection, when, unknown to them, he comes to his disciples at Emmaus and is recognized by them only when seated at the table and pronouncing the blessing at the breaking of the bread. The manner in which the artist depicted this head, the beard framing the chin and the full lips, the prominent cheek-bones which give breadth to the face, the heavily lidded eyes and the strong, highly-arched eyebrows, is an exact reproduction of the head shown in the painting of the Ashkenazi Jew. The only variation is that here Rembrandt lets the hair fall over the shoulders, and gives a nobler expression to the face.[46] The Jesus, too, in the "Hundred Guilder Print," a work of the same period, is given Semitic features.

Reverting, after this digression, to the Old Testament, we ask ourselves again; how has Rembrandt treated these subjects, as compared with his predecessors? Pieter Lastman, Rembrandt's instructor, had painted at one time "The Reconciliation of David and Absalom" (fig. 39). To understand this scene we must briefly recall the preliminary narration in the Second Book of Samuel, chapters 13 and 14. This recounts the story of Amnon, a son of the king, who became enamored of his half-sister, Tamar, and of her unwilling seduction. To avenge the wrong done his sister, her older brother, Absalom, encompassed the death of Amnon and brought down upon himself the wrath of his father, David. Later, when David had recovered from his grief at the death of his son, he yearned for Absalom, who also desired to behold his father again. "He came," the Bible tells us, "to the king and bowed himself on his face to the ground before

39. Pieter Lastman, "The Reconciliation of David and Absalom." Painting.

the king; and the king kissed Absalom." Lastman made an impressive picture of this scene. The king, with his golden caftan and high turban, is shown as an Oriental. He stands in fatherly dignity, but with no indication of sternness. His face lies in shadow and he directs a searching glance toward his son. Absalom has placed his richly plumed hat upon the ground, and has bent his knee before his father, his arms folded, in acknowledgment of his guilt. The towering ruins of a palace and, farther in the background, the outlines of a city, indicate the proximity of Jerusalem.

120

40.   Rembrandt, "The Reconciliation of David and Absalom."   Painting.

Rembrandt has given us a painting on the same theme (fig. 40); but how different is the treatment! Whereas Lastman presents his two figures in a contrasting dramatic pose, Rembrandt merges them into a single group. The painter does not even show the face of Absalom. He is content to indicate in the portrayal of the back of this man the sobs that are shaking him. There is in this painting only one pair of eyes, those of the father, which look down upon his son with an affectionate and forgiving glance. Instead of an intense pathos, every phase of the scene is softened down and, in this modulation, given a more intimate character. Lastman's figures are posed as actors upon a stage; while Rembrandt has created human beings into whose presence we come without their being aware of our approach.

We come now to another scene, this time without making a comparison with the work of another artist. It is "Abraham's Sacrifice" (fig. 41). This theme had been frequently used in Christian and also in Jewish art. It is found upon the walls of the synagogue of Dura-Europos and in the mosaic floor of the synagogue of Beth-Alpha. One may well note that our emotions are left untouched by these representations, while our sympathies are deeply stirred in contemplating the Rembrandt portrayal.

In this painting Rembrandt has given careful attention to the traditional ritual. The knife in the hand of the Patriarch is not a pointed blade, but is rounded at the tip, inasmuch as in the Jewish sacrificial rite the victim was not dispatched with a stab, but with a cut across the throat, the while the sacrificer shall "lay his hand upon the head of the burnt-offering," as directed in Leviticus 1.4.

122

41.   Rembrandt, "Abraham's Sacrifice."   Painting.

This is the gesture that Rembrandt has chosen for his painting. It is, however, the human rather than the ritualistic treatment that conveys the strong impression produced by this work. The placing of the father's hand upon the face of the youth gives us the feeling that Abraham does not wish to look upon the trusting eyes of his son. Thus, and only in this manner, can the command of the Almighty be carried out. In the culminating moment of this episode, as the knife is raised for the sacrifice, God manifests His intervention. "And the angel of the Lord called unto him out of heaven, and said: Abraham, Abraham! And he said: Here am I. And he said: Lay not thy hand upon the lad, neither do thou anything unto him." In the Bible the angel is represented only as speaking, but Rembrandt shows him as a figure in action. He accompanies the spoken words with his left arm uplifted while with the right hand he grasps the wrist of Abraham with such violence that the knife falls from the old man's hand.

In some instances, Rembrandt, in the psychological analysis of his subject, overstepped the prescribed conventional limitations, as, for example, in an etching depicting Joseph and the wife of Potiphar. The woman is not only nude, but given a wanton pose, for the purpose of intensifying the seductive power she is exerting. The artist does not regard Joseph as simply the noble and virtuous youth who would inherently resent any suggestion of this kind. Rather, one detects in his features the torment he endures before he succeeds in overcoming the temptation and fleeing from the scene. As a matter of fact, a Jewish legend, mentioned already in the Talmud (B. Sotah

124

36b), heightens the drama of the story of Joseph by saying that he had been all but led astray and was saved only through the appearance before him of a vision of his father, which recalled him to the path of virtue. Rembrandt may well have become acquainted with this legend through his Jewish friends. It may, however, have been due to the depth of his own insight into human nature which led him to give this scene so thoroughly human an interpretation.

Of special interest, in this connection, is the Rembrandt etching of "Adam and Eve" (fig. 42). Artists have, as a rule, presented our first parents as fashioned in the image of the Creator, and endowed them with a distinctive beauty. Rembrandt, however, depicts Adam as a most unattractive man, and Eve, if possible, as a still homelier woman, with heavily-shadowed eyes, a short neck, a protruding abdomen, the distortion of which is even further emphasized by the dark shadow cast upon it. The serpent forms a fitting pendant to this treatment. From ancient tradition of Jewish inception, the serpent is shown as moving about on its legs, as the command that it should crawl on its belly was pronounced by the Almighty after the commission of its sin.[47] From its back there sprout the wings of bats, the attribute of the Devil. An ancient Jewish conception, subsequently adopted by Christian writers, identified the serpent of the Paradise narrative with Satan. How repellent is here the maw of this creature, from which a few bristling hairs are sprouting, and its fangs! The fig which hangs from the reptile's jaws gives a still more repulsive touch to this feature.

What the etching loses in beauty is offset by Rembrandt's

125

42. Rembrandt, "Adam and Eve." Etching.

psychological understanding of the biblical story. The artist was clearly the first to propound to himself the question as to the character which these persons should be represented as possessing; they, who, in all the richness of Paradise, disobeyed the command of God merely to taste the forbidden fruit. They must have been primitive and inarticulate people, following only a sensual urge, and it is this conception that has been portrayed by the artist.

In contrast to the stark repulsiveness of this picture we purposely turn to a work of unusual beauty (fig. 44). It is the scene of Daniel's vision of the ram at the river Ulai (Daniel 8): "And I lifted up mine eyes, and saw, and, behold, there stood before the stream a ram which had two horns ... but one was higher than the other ...." And Daniel heard the voice which said: " 'Gabriel, make this man to understand the vision.' So he came near where I stood; and when he came I was terrified, and fell upon my face ...." Here the artist provided a different treatment from that shown in the "Adam and Eve." Every detail is softened and mellowed. The weird figure of the ram on the opposite shore of the stream is plunged in shadow. Daniel is not shown as falling upon his face in terror; only his bowed body and bent knees indicate his troubled spirit. The high light of this picture centers upon the angel who stands before us, garbed in shimmering white raiment, a brightly colored scarf draped about him. The blond hair glistens with golden tints and the white wings are far outspread. This is an angel such as children dream of. Tenderly he touches Daniel's shoulder, and with a gentle gesture of his outstretched arm directs his glance to the vision on the shore.

127

43. Rembrandt, "The Vision of Daniel." Drawing.

44.   Rembrandt, "The Vision of Daniel."   Painting.

Rembrandt always went to extremes in his art, in the coarse as in the tender, in the unattractive as well as in the beautiful.

It may be added that Rembrandt in his paintings often leaned towards the moderate and lovely, while his etchings, with less constraint, and therefore with greater directness, depicted the blunt or more repellent aspects of life. This would, naturally, not apply to all the periods of his artistic productivity; for Rembrandt in his early days went to extremes even in his paintings. But all in all this observation will be found correct, and is readily explainable. Etchings and engravings are not displayed upon walls for everyone to see, but are preserved by collectors in portfolios, and are only occasionally brought to view. The shameless woman of the Potiphar picture, the greedy figures of Adam and Eve, are etchings, not paintings. Rembrandt at one time painted the scene, so often presented in the world of art, of Abraham sending Hagar into the wilderness after Sarah had given birth to Isaac (fig. 45). Here Hagar is shown, suffused in light, seated upon an ass, the bridle of which is held in the hand of her son Ishmael. The Patriarch has accompanied her to the city gates, and with a dignified gesture points the way into the distance.

In the etching of this theme, however, the action is given a more genial treatment (fig. 46). The house is covered with ivy, while an emaciated, toothless old woman observes from a window, with evident pleasure, the departure of her young rival. Abraham is clearly a distinguished Oriental in attitude and appearance. His arms are lifted in blessing, and he appears to be uncertain whether to remain

45.   Rembrandt, "The Dismissal of Hagar." Painting.

46. Rembrandt, "The Dismissal of Hagar." Etching.

where he is or to re-enter his house. This dignified pose is, however, offset by the behavior of Hagar. She has been weeping, and now, holding her kerchief to her face, blowing her nose, tries to hide the signs of her intense emotion.

132

A similar interweaving of solemn and ordinary human traits appears in Rembrandt's etching, "Abraham Entertaining the Three Angels" (fig. 47). The angel, intended here to represent God himself, is accompanied by two others. They reveal themselves to the Patriarch at the noon hour to announce that a son will be born to him. But of more importance to the artist in this design is the entertainment provided by Abraham for his guests. God is shown seated in Oriental posture, with legs bent under, and joyously holding aloft a beaker of wine. The angel at the right of God is a bald-pated man with a black, turned-up mustache, surely no commonplace representation of a heavenly messenger. Abraham is a tremulous old man, bowed in humility, but holding in readiness, at the same time, a pewter can filled with sweet wine.

One should not conclude that Rembrandt, in creating etchings of this kind, was lacking in piety. Only an individual untroubled in his devout faith would venture upon so intimate a portrayal of the sacred figures of the Scriptures.

When we come, finally, to the drawings, we find that numerically they represent the most important portion of Rembrandt's artistic output of Old Testament incidents, and hundreds of these drawings are still in existence. A variety of incentives may account for Rembrandt's absorption in this technique. Some of these drawings may have taken form in the artist's imagination at the moment of reading the scriptural narration. This was the case in the 19th century with another Dutch painter, Vincent van Gogh, who, in a letter to his brother Theo, wrote: "Last week, I read in Genesis 23, the description

47. Rembrandt, "Abraham Entertaining the Three Angels." Etching.

of the burial of Sarah in the field that Abraham had bought for her internment in the cave of Machpelah, and instinctively I made a little drawing of the place as it appeared to me. It is not worth much, but I enclose it herewith." A few weeks later, van Gogh, influenced by the reading of First Kings, wrote: "While I am reading I now and then make a little sketch, like the one I sent you recently; and I made one this morning of Elijah in the desert, with the stormy sky and some thorn-bushes in the foreground. It is nothing special, but I see it vividly before me ...."[48] We feel that Rembrandt might have written in a similar vein, if it had been the custom in those days to indite letters of so intimate a nature.

To cite an example: we observe in the "Finding of the Infant Moses" (fig. 48), how Rembrandt had rapidly, with a few strokes of the pen, graphically reproduced the impression made upon him by the biblical narrative: "And the daughter of Pharaoh came down to bathe in the river; and her maidens walked along by the river-side; and she saw the ark among the flags, and sent her handmaid to fetch it." Pharaoh's daughter is revealed as standing with attractive grace and at the same time in a pose of regal dignity on the shore of the stream, while one of her attendants bends down and the other stoops to grasp the ark. The eye receives this threefold grouping as one continued action. Only a Chinese artist could effect such momentary movements with such economy of line.

It is probable that some of the other drawings owe their inception to his contacts with his son Titus, the only one of his children who did not die in infancy. When he grew older, Titus supplemented his

48. Rembrandt, "The Finding of the Child Moses." Drawing.

42.   Rembrandt, "The Farewell of Tobias."   Drawing.

art-dealing profession with the production of paintings, and may have recognized in his early years the hidden treasures existing in biblical narratives. Rembrandt, in relating these stories to his son, may have accompanied his talks with hasty sketches in an effort to awaken the talent which the latter might possess. These drawings of Rembrandt's include a large number of scenes from the life of Tobias. The artist found appropriate material for stirring a youthful talent in the adventurous career of a young man who goes out into the world under the continued guardianship of an angel.

What a profound sympathy, for example, is revealed in the episode of Tobias's leave-taking from his parents (fig. 49). The aged father embraces his son and presses a loving kiss upon his lips. The mother looks on, bowed down with years and sorrow. At the left is seen the waiting angel Raphael. He has no wings, since the Bible never mentions wings when describing an angel, a messenger of God. He is merely an attractive youth with flowing hair, turning his head toward the scene of farewell the while his feet seem pointed for departure. This figure is shown full front to the beholder, emphasizing its dignity; and the large walking-staff appears to be giving the signal, "Let us go!"[49]

There is another drawing in which Tobias and the angel are seen on their journey (fig. 50). The trunk of a tree leaning toward the left indicates the direction in which the group is moving. The little dog at the front has evidently outrun the travelers; one may imagine it as always running ahead and returning to its master, as dogs are wont to do. There follow, stepping gaily forward, Tobias

138

50.   Rembrandt, "Tobias and the Angel on the Journey."   Drawing.

and the angel, the latter with lifted wings. Tobias is garbed for travel, wearing stout boots, a hat upon his head, a bundle on his back, and a mountain-stick across his shoulder. The angel, however, is barefooted, his head is uncovered and his garment is airy and light; he is not subject to human requirements.

Other drawings of Rembrandt's, however, may have been designed for the instruction of his many pupils. It is probable that the master directed them to undertake some specific exercise in order to develop their talent in composition, and knew that no themes were more appropriate to this end than those provided in the Bible, with which, in those days, everyone was familiar. He may, indeed, when pupils came to him with their drawings, have sketched the scenes himself, to illustrate for them how the work was to be fashioned.

Only a few of the drawings still in existence are preliminary studies for paintings. Might this be due to the fact that so large a number of Rembrandt's paintings have disappeared, or that Rembrandt destroyed these preliminary studies after they had achieved their purpose? At any rate, a few examples of this work have survived and enable us to follow the method adopted by the artist in producing his works, from their inception to their completion.

In connection with "The Vision of Daniel," referred to in the foregoing, there exists an experimental pen-and-wash drawing (fig. 43). This drawing, in the main, gives all the details of the finished work, the kneeling Daniel, the angel, the stream, the ram. In the group showing Tobias and the angel, the sketch is more loosely composed.

140

The angel's directing arm is given a higher posture and a farther reach; in the painting it is brought nearer to the head. There is a change, too, in the right arm, which receives only in the painting the flowing sleeve which brings the angel into closer contact with Daniel. These are, perhaps, trivial details, but the beauty of a work of art is at times determined by nuances such as these.

When Rembrandt had completed a painting he achieved a perfection commensurate with his capacity at the moment, but only at the moment. His imagination was quickly reborn and he evolved new drawings that paved the way to another painting or etching. Despite the extended scope of Rembrandt's biblical themes, there are several to which he faithfully returned in an unrelaxed striving toward perfection.

One is tempted, in a few instances of Rembrandt's biblical work, to associate their content with incidents in the painter's life. When, in 1634, he married Saskia van Uylenburgh, a wealthy orphan of socially prominent parentage, he provoked dissension with his wife's relatives. They felt that this son of a miller had married out of his class and reproached him with having dissipated his wife's fortune in the purchase of ornaments and other trumpery. Rembrandt brought suit in the local court, asking for damages for the insults to which he had been subjected; but, in 1638, the case was dismissed. In the same year Rembrandt created a painting that, so far as I am aware, has never been done by anyone else. It is "Samson's Wedding" (fig. 51). Samson is, in this painting, the only Israelite, while the bride and all the participants are Philistines. Rembrandt introduces a couple of scoundrelly physiognomies among the Philistines, and they are pictured as behaving in most unmannerly fashion toward their women. Is it possible that he resorted to such a method of ventilating his anger against these estranged relatives?

This picture also bears witness to the importance placed by Rembrandt upon cultural-historical detail in his work, in an effort at a more intense realism. Samson, here, has propounded a riddle to the thirty male guests at his wedding. If they gave a correct solution they were to receive thirty changes of garment, and, if they failed, they were to present him with thirty such garments. Not being adept at figuring, as was the case in ancient days, Samson uses his fingers to aid him, and has just reached the third in his reckoning. Some of the guests are not seated, but are lounging on cushions, a meal-time custom of Antiquity. The bride is ceremonially seated in front of a tapestry, her hair loosened, and a coronet upon her head. This was the manner in which a Jewish bride was arrayed upon her wedding day. We have noted the flowing hair and the coronet in the etching of "The Great Jewish Bride" (fig. 24). The fashion also obtained among Christians, especially in rural districts;[50] but, in this instance, Rembrandt's intention is the portrayal of the ritual observed at a Jewish marriage. This has a bearing upon the presence of the single large beaker placed on a flower-wreathed plate. To this day the bride and bridegroom at a Jewish wedding drink from a single cup of wine in the course of the ceremony.

At an earlier time, shortly after his marriage, Rembrandt had painted the scene (fig. 52) in which Samson rails at his father-in-law

142

51.   Rembrandt, "Samson's Wedding."   Painting.

52.   Rembrandt, "Samson Threatening his Father-in-Law."   Painting.

who is barring his access to his wife (Judges 15.1–2). The father-in-law of Rembrandt was no longer living at the time of his marriage to Saskia; but the anger portrayed on the features of Samson, in which we find some resemblance to those of Rembrandt, may well represent his own feelings of resentment against his haughty relatives.

There is one picture, that may touch upon a phase of Rembrandt's life, which has presented many a problem to critical investigation (fig. 53). A woman of middle age is shown seated upon a bench with a book on her lap. A boy with folded hands is nestling against her. He is evidently being instructed in his first prayer. At the left, in the background, a young married couple is kneeling before an old man, who is holding an infant in his arms, evidently the child of the young couple. The picture was formerly regarded as representing Hannah with the child Samuel (I Samuel 1), in which case the parents in the background would be Elkanah and Hannah, who are bringing their first-born to the Temple of Shiloh. Today one usually identifies the boy in this picture with the youthful Timothy, who later accompanied the Apostle Paul, and his grandmother Lois, from whom Timothy had inherited his devout faith (II Timothy 1.5).[51] In this interpretation the little scene in the background could only suggest the representation of the infant Jesus in the Temple at Jerusalem.

It seems to us more correct to trace the subject of this picture to the Old Testament episode. Of course, if Hannah and Samuel should be depicted in the foreground and again at the back, it would be a double portrayal, a usage of an earlier period, not found in the

145

other works of Rembrandt. It is just here, however, that we are aided by our acquaintance with the incidents of Rembrandt's life. Saskia had borne him a son, Titus, and had died shortly thereafter. A widow, Geertge Dircx, came into his home and took motherly care of the boy. She may have really regarded herself as his mother, as Rembrandt is known to have made her an offer of marriage, a promise that was voided by him after the appearance of the youthful Hendrickje Stoffels, who gradually supplanted her in his affection. Geertge Dircx probably taught the lad his prayers, and may even have harbored the wish that he should one day enter the ministry. Thus she might have compared herself with the biblical Hannah who had consecrated her son, Samuel, to the priesthood.

That the beautiful boy in this picture was Rembrandt's son, Titus, is indicated by his age and by the resemblance to other paintings of the youth. In like manner the woman may be the Geertge Dircx, who in 1648, the year in which the painting was made, was still a member of Rembrandt's household. She was, however, as was often the case with his models, disguised in biblical garb. She was Geertge Dircx with Titus and, at the same time, Hannah with the child Samuel. In order to have this dualistic process understood, the painter has drawn both these figures together with the father again in the background as they appear in the scene of the Temple at Shiloh.[52]

It is this Temple, not that of Jerusalem, which Rembrandt shows us. Its period is quite close to the time of Moses, and for this reason it is adorned with the two tablets of the Law. Here, too, Rembrandt

146

53.   Rembrandt, "Hannah and Samuel in the Temple at Shiloh."   Painting.

has introduced, as he was often inclined to do, letters of the Hebrew alphabet. A serpent is shown between the tablets, twining about a staff. We remember this symbol from the picture of the Oriental Jew (fig. 18), the brazen serpent that had been erected by Moses to bring healing to those who had been bitten by snakes. The Bible tells us explicitly that this brazen serpent had been preserved as a sacred relic, and that not until centuries had passed was it destroyed in the Temple of Jerusalem at the time of King Hezekiah who took the field against all idols (II Kings 18.4). Rembrandt assumed that the symbol was still intact in the Temple of Shiloh. It therefore seems reasonable to us to include this picture in our group of Old Testament portrayals, and to regard it, at the same time, as peculiarly identified with incidents of Rembrandt's life.

One must, of course, be on one's guard against the inclination to find a biographical suggestion in nearly every one of his biblical pictures. It is probable that many of these were painted in response to commissions, the artist also having had frequent orders for pictures of scenes from the New Testament or from ancient history. In this manner the Stadtholder, Prince Frederick Henry of Orange, had requested him to paint a series of pictures illustrating scenes from the Passion of Christ, and a Sicilian art collector had given him a commission for classic representations of Homer, Aristotle and Alexander the Great. No one hesitated, in those days, to clip the wings of an artist by giving him a binding contract, instead of selecting from his atelier something the artist had produced from his own impulse.

148

But even if Rembrandt had been allowed to fashion his biblical pictures in line with his own intentions, not all would have borne any relation to the incidents of his own life; for it is the special endowment of the great creative artist to experience even extraneous happenings with such intensity as though they were his very own.

In one respect, as a matter of course, every work of art reflects its creator. It provides the artistic style that sways him at the moment. Inasmuch as Rembrandt's Old Testament pictures traverse his entire creative output, we intend to furnish at the conclusion of this discussion a few examples of the manner in which the Rembrandt of the early, the middle and the later period apprehended and painted the biblical themes. This will provide us with an opportunity of acquainting ourselves with several other paintings, etchings and drawings and thus enlarge our understanding of the artist's relation to the Bible.

The twenty-year-old Rembrandt, while yet residing in Leyden, painted the first of his still-existing biblical pictures, "Tobit and his Wife" (fig. 54). The theme is here presented with a precision of detail as though the world were a microscopic slide, and the artist held a microscope in his hand. The home in which these two persons dwell, though narrow as a bird-cage, is crowded with all manner of domestic furnishing. To indicate the poverty of the old man, he painted the toes that protrude from the worn-out shoes; and every wrinkle of the woman's face is shown. But Rembrandt's genial spirit sparkles even through his pedantic accuracy. The incident chosen is the moment in which the woman enters the room with a

54. Rembrandt, "Tobit and his Wife." Painting.

kid, and the old man, made mistrustful by his blindness, suspects his wife of having stolen the animal. The indignation and amazement of the woman at this misapprehension on the part of her old life-partner are strikingly revealed in the angry glare of her wide-open eyes.

Arrived in Amsterdam, Rembrandt discarded the restricted scope of his earlier work. His pictures had been produced in a small format; now he used a larger canvas. The free atmosphere of the metropolis developed and enflamed the artist's temperament, and he turned eagerly to dramatic themes as subjects for his paintings. We show, for example, his "Belshazzar's Feast" (fig. 55). It is the story told in the fifth chapter of the Book of Daniel, presented in the masterly manner of which these biblical narrators were capable. Here is recorded the splendor of the royal feast, the haughty bearing of the king as he commands his servants to fetch the golden vessels his father had stolen from the Temple of Jerusalem, the sudden hush of the tumult at the feast as a hand is seen writing on the wall the mysterious words *Mene, Mene, Tekel, Upharsin*. "Then the king's countenance was changed in him, and his thoughts affrighted him; and the joints of his loins were loosed and his knees smote one against another."

Rembrandt portrays this scene at the high point of its dramatic tension. A circle of light irradiates the Hebrew script, with the letters of which he is so familiar. They appear in five rows of three letters each, to be read from the top to the bottom. The king has jumped up from his seat at the table on which the golden vessels

55. Rembrandt, "Belshazzar's Feast." Painting.

56. Rembrandt, "The Blinding of Samson." Painting.

of the Temple are lying. Of no avail now is his gold-brocaded robe or the beautifully folded turban, surmounted by his crown. He is stricken with terror at sight of the pallid, ghostly hand that emerges out of the shadow. Conscious of guilt, he stretches his right hand to grasp one of the vessels, upsetting a beaker, the contents of which flow on the table. At his right, a female servant had just approached with a pitcher filled with wine, but now steps back affrighted, so that here, too, the wine streams from the vessel.

Rembrandt, at this time, had selected from the story of Samson, for which he had a great affection, its most harrowing incident. It is the moment when Samson, after his hair had been shorn and his strength gone from him, was blinded by the Philistines (fig. 56). Uncannily, as though in a nightmare, the gruesome action is consummated. The hair is cut off; and Delilah, the shears in her right hand, and the shock of hair in her left, is fleeing from the tent. The fallen man attempts to kick her, but fails to do so. The Philistines, pictured as dwarfish, goblin-like creatures, have thrown themselves upon the herculean Samson, and are thrusting their weapons into his eyes. One might wish that less cruelty had been depicted by the artist; but this was a period of hardy nerves, and artists, painters and poets furnished their public with a pabulum supplied in our days by the motion-picture: the exciting, the breath-taking.

"Abraham's Sacrifice," described in these pages (fig. 41), was produced in this decade, and also revealed the artist's leaning toward the sensational. The sacrificial knife has already been poised, and had not the angel stormed upon the scene at this moment and thrust back the uplifted hand of Abraham, the sacrifice would have been consummated.

In the story of Tobit, he seized the moment in which the angel, having safely brought back the youth and restored the health of the father, departs from the family (fig. 57). Here, also, Rembrandt knows how to produce a striking scene. He shows the angel taking rapid flight, with wings outspread, arms extended, the legs in motion and the raiment whirling in the wind. This rapid leave-taking throws all the members of the family into a state of agitation. The father Tobit falls in adoration to the ground; the son, kneeling, gazes entranced aloft. The wife of the aged Tobit turns shyly away from the heavenly apparition; the daughter-in-law peers timidly, but with curiosity, at the departing figure. Even the little dog is an interested participant; it cowers in fear, while barking at the heavenly messenger.

Only a few years separated this picture from one of Rembrandt's most alluring creations, "Manoah's Sacrifice" (fig. 58). An unknown man has appeared to Manoah and his wife, announcing to them the approaching birth of a son. To honor the bearer of the tidings for this promise, the two old people make a burnt-offering to the Almighty, and "when the flame went up toward heaven from off the altar, the angel of the Lord ascended in the flame of the altar; and Manoah and his wife looked on, and they fell on their faces to the ground." The theme, here, is similar to the one used in the Tobit picture, the departure of an angel from the sight of mortals. But with what a moderation of treatment is this incident given! The only emphatic gesture is the agitation shown in the uplifted hands

155

57.   Rembrandt, "The Angel Leaving Tobias and his Family."   Painting.

58. Rembrandt, "Manoah's Sacrifice." Painting.

of Manoah and the head turning away in fear of the revelation which is only now recognized to have been divine in character. "We shall surely die, because we have seen God," are the words which the Bible has him speak. His wife, on the other hand, remains immobile as a statue. Her calmness stems from her deep faith in God's goodness and grace. She bends in prayer, with her knees close together and with clasped fingers; the head is slightly lowered and the eyes are closed. Her face, of distinctly Jewish cast, reveals an unshakable faith. The angel is without wings. He is shown in a white garment, gently ascending, as though rising from the haze of the burnt-offering. In the place of a Baroque agitation we are here presented with a Classic tranquillity. Italian art, with its harmony, along with the sedateness that comes with maturity, have brought an evident moderation to the artist's approach to his work.

Impelled by this tendency toward tranquillity and moderation, Rembrandt now gives a variant to the theme of Abraham's Sacrifice, which he had in the earlier treatment depicted with such dramatic tension (fig. 41). The etching (fig. 59), designed in 1655, exactly twenty years after the painting, associates Abraham, Isaac and the angel in a placid grouping. The angel is not in flight to the scene and makes no outcry. The pose is that of one standing and speaking. His left hand grasps the arm that holds the knife; the other hand strives with Abraham's right which covers the eyes of the boy.

It is understandable that the drawings of the late and latest periods should also manifest this tendency toward moderation. As an example, one may examine the scene of "Nathan Reprimanding

158

59.   Rembrandt, "Abraham's Sacrifice."   Etching.

David" (fig. 60). The prophet is reproaching the king for having sent Uriah, the husband of the beautiful Bathsheba, to his death in order to gain possession of her without hindrance. Rembrandt here avoided any dramatic portrayal of the episode. Nathan is no passionate zealot, but a wizened old and troubled man who bases his accusation only upon the principle of justice. David is seated facing him, ensconced upon a splendidly caparisoned couch, and is regally attired. But, hesitating to bring his own power into play, he listens humbly to the words of the prophet, in self-reproach for his transgressions. This magnificent narrative, one of the loveliest gems of the Bible, could not have been given a simpler treatment than is found in this drawing. It is probable that it served Rembrandt as a preliminary sketch for a painting that has not survived to our day.[53]

Returning again to a consideration of the paintings, Rembrandt, in 1655, the same year in which the etching of "Abraham's Sacrifice" was made, painted the scene of "Potiphar's Wife Accusing Joseph" (fig. 61). With what tension would the young artist have endowed the incidents of this episode: a traducing woman, an infuriated husband, a youth passionately protesting his innocence! The master provided us, in his fifties, with but a minimum of excitement. He suggests the accusation of the woman by a mere movement of the thumb of her right hand. The left is pressed against her breast in solemn asseveration of her honor. Joseph raises only his left hand and his head. God alone knows where the truth lies. Potiphar is shown as unattractive, slender and negligible. Did Rembrandt desire to convey the impression that he is too anemic for this woman?[54]

160

60. Rembrandt, "Nathan Reprimanding David." Drawing.

61. Rembrandt, "Potiphar's Wife Accusing Joseph." Painting.

In the economy of movement employed, as a result of the limited dramatic treatment, the eye is more directly attracted to the technical values of the production — to the white sheets on the bed, the golden-brown counterpane, the striped rose-colored gown of the woman, to the bluish-gray cloak of Joseph on which the woman has placed her foot. The colors are, here, in contrast to the artist's smoother treatment in his earlier years, laid more heavily and visibly on the canvas. They seem, at times, to diffuse a glorious radiance.

In the following year he gave us a new masterpiece (fig. 62). Joseph has brought his two sons — the elder, Manasseh, and the younger, Ephraim — to his old, half-blinded father Jacob, that these may receive his blessing before his death. Jacob has placed his right hand, which radiates a greater strength for the blessing, upon the head of the younger son, and the left upon the elder. Joseph, desirous that the more important blessing be bestowed upon his first-born, cautiously endeavors to direct the hand of his father toward the head of the other child, but the old man will not be diverted from his purpose.

This is the treatment designed by the artist; but it will be understood only by one familiar with the biblical text. Rembrandt was no longer as eager a narrator as he had been in the past, and was not as intent upon stressing the intensity of an action as he was to evoke the mood in which it was carried out. The solemn blessing bestowed by a venerable Patriarch and its humble acceptance by a golden-haired lad provide the impressive motif to which every other detail is subordinated. Even the inanimate objects, the folds of the

163

curtains, the heavy fur that droops from Jacob's shoulder seem to reflect the reverential temper that permeates the picture.

The biblical narrative does not mention Joseph's wife in this incident, and Jewish legend has, therefore, been called upon to explain her presence. In the moment of bestowing the blessing upon his two grandsons, Jacob sees in a prophetic vision that their descendants, Kings Jehu and Jeroboam, will be idol-worshippers. Thereupon he hesitates and, turning to his son, asks whether his marriage to the Egyptian woman, Asenath, has been legally contracted. Joseph calls his wife to his side, produces the contract of marriage, and says: "I pray thee, my father, bless my sons, if only for the sake of this pious woman. . . ." Whereupon Jacob proceeds with the blessing.[55] Our attention has so frequently been directed to Rembrandt's interest in Jewish matters, that his acquaintance with this legend seems very probable to us. The story could have been conveyed to him by the person who ordered the picture, who may, in this instance, have been a Jew and have requested the painter to be sure to include this figure in his work.

The picture of "Jacob Wrestling with the Angel,"[56] also a product of these years, does not represent a conflict, but, rather, a benediction (fig. 63). Although the angel is shown thrusting his right leg and his left hand against Jacob, dislocating the latter's hip, he is, at the same time, looking down at him benignantly, granting the plea of Jacob: "I will not let thee go, except thou bless me." As a mother enfolds her child, the angel holds the head of Jacob, whose shadowed face is silhouetted against the white garment of the

164

62.   Rembrandt, "Jacob Blessing his Grandchildren."   Painting.

angel. The towering wings of the latter enfold both figures as in a niche.

Moses holding aloft the two tables of the Law (fig. 64) is not the Moses who angrily breaks the tablets as he surprises the people dancing about the golden calf. He is here the Moses who for the second time comes from the mountain, carrying the new tablets. "And it came to pass, when Moses came down from Mount Sinai with the two tables of the testimony in Moses' hand, when he came down from the mount, that Moses knew not that the skin of his face sent forth beams while He talked with him." The Hebrew word for emitting rays also signifies acquiring horns, and in the older art, which was based upon the Latin translation of the Bible, the Vulgate, Moses was generally depicted with a pair of horns. The Rembrandt picture, also, leans more to the concept of horns than of rays. At the same time, Rembrandt adds a shimmering glow to the face.

In the days that Rembrandt was at work upon this painting, a colleague of his, Ferdinand Bol, was commissioned to paint a Moses for the newly erected Town Hall in Amsterdam. This was a large canvas on which Moses is shown in full figure standing on Mount Sinai with the tablets of the Law he is bringing to the people — here, too, they are the second tablets. Regarding this painting, the question has been asked whether Rembrandt had originally been requested to undertake this work which, for some reason or other, had not been accepted.[57] In the case of another painting, also intended for the Town Hall — this depicts the conspiracy of Julius Civilis — Rembrandt had a similar experience, the picture failing to meet the

166

63.   Rembrandt, "Jacob Wrestling with the Angel."   Painting.

approval of the authorities. If this conjecture is correct, it may also be asked whether the original treatment by Rembrandt had been more comprehensive, perhaps including the multitude at the foot of the mountain. Rembrandt's existing picture, however, appeals to us as completely satisfying as we have it, inasmuch as its entire interest is concentrated upon the figure of Moses.

Remarkable, also, is the fact that the nearer of the two tablets which Moses is holding aloft, contains, not the first five of the Commandments, but the last five. May this have been due to the fact that in the room selected for this painting a companion-piece was to be placed, also a Moses — the one depicting his first descent from the mountain — on the tablets of which the first five Commandments were to be shown, so that the two pictures might provide a complete presentation of the Law? Or may it have seemed more important to those who had commissioned the work that the moral injunctions of the Commandments, included in the sixth to the tenth, be given a greater emphasis than those of the first five, which relate to the proper worship of God and forbid the making of graven images, an inhibition not binding upon Christians? Rembrandt has here again, as he had so often, introduced the Hebrew words with meticulous care.

This, too — that is, the manner in which the tablets are raised — seems to me the result of Jewish influence. Certainly Rembrandt must at some time or other have been present at a Jewish religious service and he must have seen there how the scroll of the Torah, after having been used for reading, is lifted up with the words: "And this is the Law which Moses set before the children of Israel ..."

168

64. Rembrandt, "Moses Lifting the Tablets of the Law." Painting.

This ceremonial act may have impressed Rembrandt so that he took it over into his picture of Moses.

Let us, finally, place in juxtaposition two pictures of the master's earlier and later periods, both treating the same episodes — the young David playing the harp before the mentally-unbalanced Saul. The latter has fallen into a state of melancholy after he had been abandoned by Samuel and the star of his glory had dimmed. He found comfort only in the music of the harp, so masterfully rendered by the youthful David. But after the latter had slain the giant, Goliath, and had, for this achievement, been universally acclaimed, the king grew jealous and planned his death. It is this moment that the earlier Rembrandt had chosen for portrayal (fig. 65). David strikes the strings of the harp with mobile fingers, and even the ornately curved framework of the harp seems to have something restless in its outlines. Saul grasps, while listening, a long and sinister-looking spear and glances mistrustfully toward the youth. There hovers over the scene a sense of imminent catastrophe.

In his later work (fig. 66), Rembrandt picked a calmer scene. David, still in the king's favor, plays before him, and "Saul found relief, and it was well with him, and the evil spirit departed from him" (I Samuel 16.23). Here, as in the case of "Jacob's Blessing," everything is concentrated about one central mood — in this case it is pain. The king has been moved to the depths of his soul by the music. His madness dissolves in tears. Tears fall from his eyes, and he grasps at the nearest object, the curtain at his back, to dry them. A fold of the curtain covers the left eye; the right is open,

170

revealing the more clearly the grief that assails him. The effect, here, is emphasized in the contrast afforded by the splendor of the king's apparel. He wears a gold-brocaded robe, a purple cloak, a white turban braided with red and sea-green strands, surmounted by a small silver crown. But what avails all this grandeur if the spirit is darkened with sorrow?

Let us glean again from an examination of this picture, the last one in our gallery, the theory propounded in our analyses of the other pictures. In the first place, Rembrandt utilizes here, too, models whose Jewishness is unmistakable. The king is a slender man, with curved nose and a black beard, in whose countenance are graven lines of melancholy that appear to be permanently fixed in the features. Such an expression of sorrow is not infrequent in Jewish faces. Even in the racial lineaments of David a certain tendency to melancholy is revealed, but above all else we sense a profound preoccupation. Is he absorbed in the melodies he lures from the harp; or is he swayed by dreams of an illustrious future? For this youth who now is sitting so humbly, withdrawn into a corner, while playing upon the harp, shall one day boldly grasp an opportunity that will place him upon a royal throne![58]

It is, furthermore, just this picture that definitely belongs to those associated with the incidents of Rembrandt's personal life. It had, formerly, been included in the work of his latest years, but nowadays it is supposed to have been produced in the fifties of the 17th century. The model that posed for the king is also found in an "Adoration of the Magi," painted by Rembrandt in 1657 (London,

171

65. Rembrandt, "David Playing the Harp before Saul." Painting.

66. Rembrandt, "David Playing the Harp before Saul." Painting.

Buckingham Palace). The splendor of the king's attire would indicate that Rembrandt was still in possession of the wealth of material which had been lost to him in 1657 and 1658, at the time of his financial disaster. In the period of this threatened catastrophe the artist may have frequently labored under deep depression. But in those days he may often have experienced the emotion that swayed the spirit of King Saul as he listened to the music of David's harp: that art possessed a magic to drive away despondency. It was not necessary that he, like Saul, have some other person bring this relief to him; for he himself could take in hand the brush or the etching-needle, or the pen, and forget all his cares. In the incident of the picture under consideration he may have projected his own sorrow into the melancholy of King Saul, and have found solace in his work.

In the final years of Rembrandt's life he experienced yet further griefs. Hendrickje Stoffels, many years his junior, died seven years before his own demise, and deprived the master of the affectionate care of a woman during his last days. His only son, Titus, was a handsome, distinguished and talented man, but at the same time, delicate and ailing. He died shortly after he had married, and Rembrandt endured this additional bereavement.

In the autumn of 1669 death overtook the painter himself, mourned by only a few of his contemporaries. Among his personal possessions at the time of his death but one book is mentioned — the Bible. This Book had accompanied him from the days of his childhood until the very end. It had continuously stirred his imagination to the creation of a series of pictures, and he possessed the

174

gift of bringing into visual form the fancies that it stimulated in his mind. Never before or since Rembrandt wrought his great work has there appeared upon the stage of life an artist whose works provided such inspiring testimony to the content and power of the narratives of Holy Writ.

NOTES

[1] Filippo Baldinucci, in his book entitled *Cominciamento e progresso dell'arte d'intagliare in rame colle vite de' più eccellenti maestri della stessa professione*, Firenze, 1686, writes: "His unattractive and plebeian features were accentuated by his stained and untidy attire, it being his custom to wipe his brushes on his clothes and to be otherwise careless of his appearance." The reference here is probably to the older Rembrandt, as the youth, to judge by his self-portraits, seems to have given much care to his apparel.

[2] Compare the chapter on "Rembrandt at the Latin School," in Wilhelm R. Valentiner's book, *The Art of the Low Countries*, Garden City, N. Y., 1914.

[3] A previously reported visit to England, about 1662, is today more and more called into question. Reasons for these doubts are given by W. R. Valentiner in his *Rembrandt. Des Meisters Handzeichnungen*, II, Leipzig, 1934, p. XXIII. The more recently advanced suggestion that such a trip to England had been made about 1640 is also rightly doubted. Cf. A. Welcker in *Oud Holland*, LVII, 1940, pp. 115 ff.

[4] With a painting sent by Rembrandt, in 1639, as a gift to Constantin Huygens, secretary to the Stadtholder Prince Frederick Henry of Orange, he expressed the wishes: "that the picture should be hung . . . in such a way that the spectator may stand far enough from it to appreciate its effect from a distance." The reference is probably to the painting "The Blinding of Samson" (fig. 56).

[5] There is a tendency, among some of Rembrandt's biographers, to dramatize the story of his life. They contrast great wealth and dire poverty; a sparkling *joie de vivre*, and melancholic embitterment. The available records fail to support these assumptions. The later self-portraits of the master reveal a self-conscious dignity. The hilarity shown in the self-portrait in the Carstanjen collection, now in the Cologne Museum, cannot be interpreted as a bitter, mocking laughter, but rather as simple, honest laughter. Wolfgang Stechow, in *The Art Quarterly*, VII (1945), pp. 233 ff., designates this self-portrait as "Democritus, the Laughing Philosopher."

[6] The description of Amsterdam given by Descartes is contained in a letter written by him in 1631 to Jean Louis Guez de Balzac. Cf. Emile Michel, *Rembrandt*, London, 1895, p. 79.

[7] The picture of the peaceful conditions of life enjoyed by the Jews in Amsterdam is presented by Jacques Basnage in his *Histoire des Juifs depuis Jesus Christ jusqu'a présent*, Rotterdam, 1706 ff. I cite the English edition, London, 1708, Book 7, chap. XXXII, p. 738. A similar thought is expressed by Spinoza in his *Tractatus Theologico-politicus*, chap. XX (1670), where, referring to Amsterdam, he says: "In this flourishing state, in this magnificent city, all the inhabitants, regardless of their nationality or denomination, dwell together in a harmonious unity. . . . No one is concerned about the religious or factional associations of his neighbors, inasmuch as these distinctions play no part in the decisions handed down by the judges in the cases that come before the courts."

[8] For further details relating to the Amsterdam of that period, see Frits Lugt, *Wandelingen met Rembrandt in en om Amsterdam*, Amsterdam, 1915. Enlarged German edition, entitled, *Mit Rembrandt in Amsterdam*, Berlin, 1920.

[9] Complaint against this spirit of tolerance is registered by I. I. Schudt, *Juedische Merckwuerdigkeiten*, I, Frankfurt and Leipzig, 1714, Bk. 4, chap. 18, §4: "It is due to an all too widespread Jewish toleration in Holland that in this country, especially in Amsterdam, Christians openly and without shame accept the Jewish faith and submit to the rite of circumcision, a procedure forbidden throughout the Roman Empire, and punishable by death."

[10] In his work, *Della Pitura*, vol. III.

[11] There are a number of copies of this picture in existence. The one here reproduced has only recently come to light and is recognized as the original copy. Cf. C. H. Collins Baker, "Rembrandt's 'Thirty Pieces of Silver,'" in the *Burlington Magazine*, LXXV, 1939, pp. 179 f.

[12] This thought was expressed by Dr. Abraham Heschel of New York.

[13] The earliest known of Rembrandt's Jewish portraits is the one in Wanås, Sweden, belonging to Count Wachtmeister. It bears the date 1632, the year in which Rembrandt settled in Amsterdam. The youth with the large, round eyes is most probably a Sephardi Jew.

[14] Cf. Leone da Modena, *Historia degli Riti Hebraici*, part 1, chapter 2, section 3.

[15] An exception is provided only by the painting of medallions, also taken up by Jewish artists. Compare my article, "Jewish Artists Before the Period of Emancipation," *Hebrew Union College Annual*, XVI, 1941, pp. 366 f.

[16] This is recorded by John Colerius in his *Biography of Spinoza*. See Ernst Altkirch, *Spinoza im Portrait*, Jena, 1913, pp. 52 f.

[17] In my view, this is the identical Jew who appears in Rembrandt's pen-and-wash drawing in the Teyler Museum in Haarlem, the main feature of which is the picture of two Jews walking along a street (Lippmann-Hofstede de Groot, *Original Drawings by Rembrandt*, Berlin, 1888 ff., no. 81). The fur cap would suggest a Polish Jew, the bearing of the figure indicating a Jew of special distinction. Both these phases would fit the personality of Rabbi Moses Rivkes of Wilna, who, in 1655, fled to Amsterdam where he remained until 1661. Although an Ashkenazi Jew he enjoyed, owing to his great scholarship, the esteem and friendship of the Sephardi Rabbis, and may, therefore, have been more readily inclined to sit as a model to a painter, although not for a portrait. For a reference to Rivkes see Israel Cohen's book on *Vilna*, in the Jewish Communities Series, Philadelphia, 1943, pp. 41 ff.

[18] The long-vanished portrait in oil of Manasseh ben Israel is included as no. 841 in the Hofstede de Groot *Rembrandt Catalogue*. In the Manasseh ben Israel literature there is a certain confusion regarding the Rembrandt portraits of the Rabbi. In Lucien Wolf's *Manasseh ben Israel's Mission to Oliver Cromwell*, London, 1901, there is an 18th-century mezzotint reproduction of the Rembrandt etching. He also includes as a portrait of Manasseh a copy of the Leningrad Hermitage picture, later in the possession of C. S. Gulbenkian of Paris. It is no longer identified as a portrait of the Rabbi, as it bears no resemblance to the Rembrandt etching. Cecil Roth, in his book, *Menasseh ben Israel*, Philadelphia, 1934, p. 349, also disavows this identity, contending that it was painted in 1656, because at that time the Rabbi lay dying in Middleburg. As a matter of fact the picture had been made as early as 1645. On

178

page 109 of his book Roth erroneously gives the date of the etching as 1654, and refers to a 1645 Rembrandt portrait of Manasseh, obviously confusing this with the Hermitage-Gulbenkian portrait of 1645 which he subsequently disavows.

[19] The description appears in a biography of Manasseh ben Israel, prefacing the English translation, by P. F. (Thomas Pocock), 1780, of Manasseh's *De Termino Vitae*.

[20] This praying-shawl, the *tallit*, as worn by orthodox Jews, was drawn over the head and reached to the floor. However, as shown in the picture of the Amsterdam Sephardi Synagogue (fig. 27), the *tallit* was already at that time used in a shorter form, reaching from the hat to the middle of the body.

[21] Cf. Jacob Zwarts, "Haham Saul Levy Morteyra en zijn portret door Rembrandt," in the periodical *Oud Holland*, vol. 43, 1926, pp. 1 ff. His conclusion is refuted, on the basis of reasons given in our text, by J. S. da Silva Rosa, "Heeft Rembrandt het portret van Chagam Saul Levi Morteyra geschilderd?" in the Holland-Jewish weekly, *De Vrijdagavond*, III, 1, 1926, pp. 22 ff.

[22] Cf. the article by Mrs. J. Goekop-de-Jongh, "De Man met het vergrootglas, dor Rembrandt," in *Bredius Festbundel*, Amsterdam, 1915, pp. 53 ff.

[23] Cf. Frits Lugt, "Man with the Magnifying Glass," in *Art in America*, XXX (1942), pp. 174 ff.

[24] Cf. Jacob Zwarts, *The Significance of Rembrandt's "The Jewish Bride,"* Amersfort, 1929. In addition to the biblical interpretation of this picture there has recently been suggested a symbolic one, according to which the couple is supposed to portray connubial harmony (*Concordia Maritale*). Cf. Charles de Tolnay, "Interprétation de la 'Fiancée Juive.' " in the periodical *L'Amour de l'Art*, XVI (1935), pp. 277 ff.

[25] The well-known proprieties of Jewish life would make it unlikely that a Jew would permit himself to be portrayed in the moment of approaching his wife with such an affectionate gesture.

[26] There is an engraving of Rabbi Isaac Aboab da Fonseca (1605–1693) by Aernout Naghtegael and one of Rabbi Sasportas (1610–1698) by Pieter van Gunst, both of which are reproduced in Brugmans and Frank, *Geschiedenis der Joden in Nederland*, I, Amsterdam, 1940, facing p. 289. Two oil paintings portraying Jacob Sasportas, owned in Amsterdam, are reproduced in *De Vrijdagavond*, V, 2 (1928), pp. 132 and 134.

[27] Even before the time of the Jewish emigration from the Iberian Peninsula to Holland, a Moroccan Jew, one Samuel Pallache (died 1616) functioned here as resident consul. He was one of the founders of the first Jewish congregation. His successor in office, from 1616 to 1637, was his brother Josef. The latter's three sons, Isaac, Moses and David, were also active in Holland in the services of the King of Morocco. Rabbi Isaac ben Abraham Uziel, who officiated as head of the Nevah Shalom Sephardi Congregation from 1610 to 1622, was also a native of Morocco.

[28] This is reported by Arnold Houbraken, *De groote schouburgh der Nederlandsche konstschilders en schilderessen*, vol. I, Amsterdam, 1718.

[29] Cf. Jacob Zwarts, *The Significance of Rembrandt's "The Jewish Bride,"* p. 11.

[30] Cf. Werner Weisbach, *Rembrandt*, Berlin, 1926, p. 232, and W. R. Valentiner, *Rembrandt, Des Meisters Handzeichnungen*, II, p. 400, to no. 572.

[31] Bernard Picart, in his *Cérémonies et coutumes religieuses de tous les peuples du monde*, nouvelle édition, Amsterdam, 1789, p. 86, says: "On the day of their marriage, both bride and bridegroom array themselves as splendidly as possible. . . . The bride,

without any headdress, her hair flowing over her shoulders, is then escorted by her women friends and their daughters, with pomp and ceremony, to the house of betrothal. There she is seated between two matrons, and the younger girls adorn her with her bridal finery, of which the veil is the principal feature."

[32] In Rembrandt's picture, "The Circumcision," in the Washington National Gallery of Art, there are shown as assisting at the rite — if one disregards a youth in the left foreground — ten men in the group surrounding the mother with the infant Jesus; here, too, indicating the ritually prescribed attendance of ten men at the solemn ceremony. A "Circumcision," with the assistance of ten men, is already found in a picture by an Antwerp mannerist of the 16th century, owned by a private collector in Berlin. Reproduced by Max Friedlaender in "Die Antwerpener Manieristen," in *Jahrbuch der Preussischen Kunstsammlungen*, XXXV (1915), p. 83. Friedlaender describes this picture as a Presentation in the Temple. That it is intended to represent a circumcision is indicated by the candle that is usually introduced at this ceremony, and by the receptacle carried by the *mohel* for the instruments used at this rite.

[33] Cf. Ludwig Muenz, "Rembrandt's Synagogue and Some Problems of Nomenclature," in *The Journal of the Warburg Institute*, III (1939–40), pp. 119 ff.

[34] The large Ashkenazi Synagogue in Amsterdam, erected in 1670, was the first to provide galleries for women, evidently due to Sephardi influence.

[35] The book is entitled *Vindiciae Judaeorum* and was published in 1656. Cf. M. Kayserling, "Menasse ben Israel," in *Jahrbuch fuer die Geschichte der Juden*, II (1861), p. 112.

[36] An earlier conception of the Jewish burial-ground by Ruisdael is found in the Detroit, Mich., Institute of Art. See J. Rosenberg, "The Jewish Cemetery by Jacob van Ruisdael," in *Art in America*, XIV (1926), pp. 37 ff., and Kurt Ernst Simon, "Wann hat Ruisdael den Judenfriedhof gemalt?" in *Festschrift fuer Adolf Goldschmidt*, Berlin, 1935, pp. 158 ff.

[37] In like manner, biblical themes were tolerated in the mosaic floor-work of the synagogues of this period. It was obviously the Christian pictorial cult that in the first place had resulted in intensifying an aversion from pictorial representation among the Jews of the Middle Ages. See my book, *A History of Jewish Art*, Cincinnati, 1946.

[38] Cf. J. C. van Dyke, *Rembrandt and his School*, New York, 1922, and *The Rembrandt Drawings and Etchings*, New York and London, 1927.

[39] Otto Benesch, *Artistic and Intellectual Trends from Rubens to Daumier*, Cambridge, Mass., 1943, p. 25, suggests that the etching of the statue in the "Dream of Nebuchadnesar," in its fifth state, had been influenced by an engraving in the book by the English Hebraist, Hugh Broughton, *A Concent of Scriptures*. This is quite probable. Benesch errs, however, in adding that Manasseh ben Israel during his stay in England had come across this book and shown it to Rembrandt after his return to Holland. Menasseh had returned in a dying condition and expired at Middleburg on November 20, 1657, before reaching Amsterdam. The *Piedra Gloriosa*, at any rate, had been published in the year 5415 (1655), which was prior to Manasseh's departure for England. Broughton's book, published as early as 1588, must have been familiar to the well-read Manasseh.

[40] The name of the creator of these engravings is not given, but he was evidently a Jew, as Manasseh's experiences with a Christian artist, so far as the interpretation

180

of the Second Commandment was concerned, had been far from pleasant. It is probable that this Jew was Salom d'Italia, a copper-plate engraver whose presence in Amsterdam, from 1637 to 1660, is a matter of record (fig. 13). Cecil Roth, in his book on Manasseh, also names Salom d'Italia in this connection.

[41] Baldinucci, in the before-mentioned book (see note 1), believes that the artist was a member of a definite religious sect, the Mennonites; but there are many phases of Rembrandt's manner of living that would make this unlikely. In his artistic productions he, at any rate, evidences a Christianity that stands above all denominations and in its warm love of humanity reveals a relationship to Jewish life.

[42] It was probably under the influence of such doctrines of Jesus that Rembrandt expressed what Joachim von Sandrart, in his *Teutsche Akademie der Edlen Bau-Bild-und Mahlerey-Kunste*, I, Nuremberg, 1675, disapprovingly refers to as follows: "He manifested little regard for his position, consorting with persons of a lower class, a habit that interfered with his work." As though Rembrandt's association with the common people had not brought forth his finest works! His love for the parable of the Prodigal Son is expressed in an etching and in a painting of his later years, now in the Hermitage in Leningrad. In this painting the aged father, shown with a small cap on his head, could have been created from a Jewish model.

[43] W. R. Valentiner, *Rembrandt, Des Meisters Handzeichnungen*, I, p. IX, emphasizes the originality of Rembrandt in the selection of this scene. It was already found in the book *Neue kuenstliche Figuren biblischer Historien, gruentlich von Tobia Stimmer gerissen*, Basel, 1576.

[44] This picture of "The Danae," in the Hermitage, has also frequently been interpreted as a biblical scene: as Sarah awaiting Abraham or as Rachel awaiting Jacob. Erwin Panofsky, in his exhaustive study, "Der gefesselte Eros. Zur Genealogie von Rembrandt's Danae," in the periodical *Oud Holland*, vol. L (1933), pp. 193 ff., referring to the traditional rendering of the Danae theme, produces evidence for his contention that the picture is properly so designated.

[45] Cf. Hugo Grotius, *De Veritate Religionis Christianae*, Bk. 5, sec. 1, Amsterdam, 1644–1646.

[46] The reference is, of course, to the picture in the Louvre. The related picture in the Museum of Copenhagen, produced in the same year, does not show these Jewish features.

[47] Cf. Louis Ginzberg, *The Legends of the Jews*, I, Philadelphia, 1909, p. 71. That it was a fig-tree is based in Jewish tradition upon the phrase: "they sewed fig-leaves together and made themselves girdles" (Genesis 3.7). The elephant in the background is interpreted by Count Klaus von Baudissin in the *Repertorium fuer Kunstwissenschaft*, 45 (1925), p. 150, as a symbol of chastity. It had been previously introduced in Coornherts' engraving of 1548, which was in Rembrandt's possession.

[48] See *The Letters of Vincent van Gogh to his Brother*, I, London, Boston and New York, (1927), pp. 121 f. and p. 130.

[49] Dr. Otto Benesch, in reply to my request for his opinion regarding this drawing, writes: "Concerning your inquiry about 'The Farewell of Tobias,' I have seen the original and consider it a work of Rembrandt of the early fifties. However, only the figure group is Rembrandt's own work. The meaningless setting, transforming an interior into an out-of-doors scene, is by a pupil or copyist whose handiwork I have observed in several other drawings of the thirties or forties." Dr. Benesch is engaged

upon a new edition of *Rembrandt's Drawings* for the Phaidon Press in Oxford, England.

⁵⁰ In this fashion, with loosely flowing hair, the bride is pictured in the paintings of a peasant wedding by Pieter Breughel, the younger, in the Vienna State Museum, in the Leningrad Hermitage, and in other portrayals of this theme. Cf. Hugo Schmerber, "Rembrandt's Simsonhochzeit" in the *Kunstchronik*, new series, XVI (1904–05), col. 97 ff.

⁵¹ The identification of Timothy and his grandmother in this picture was advanced by Joh. Dyserinck in *Leidsche Jaarboekje*, 1906, p. 103 ff. That the woman against whose knees the boy is leaning represents Geertge Dircx, Rembrandt's housekeeper, and the boy his son, Titus, is assumed by W. R. Valentiner, *Rembrandt und seine Umgebung*, Strassburg, 1905, p. 37.

⁵² I am gratified to find a similar conclusion advanced by W. R. Valentiner in his article "William Drost, Pupil of Rembrandt," published in *The Art Quarterly*, II (1939), pp. 295 ff. Valentiner, to be sure, interprets the scene in the background as "The Presentation in the Temple." "This is," he writes, "an anachronism; but it is a characteristic parallelism between the story of the Old and New Testament to which the artist — or the commissioner of the painting — wanted to refer" (p. 315).

⁵³ W. R. Valentiner sees in this drawing a preliminary sketch for a picture that was designed to serve as a companion-piece to the subsequently created "David Playing the Harp before Saul" (fig. 66). See his article, "Ein Altersentwurf Rembrandt's," in the periodical *Genius*, I (1922), p. 44.

⁵⁴ The "Joseph and Potiphar" picture, in the Washington National Gallery, painted in the same year, was, undoubtedly, produced *after* the Berlin picture. The woman's gesture of the hand, with the accusing thumb directed toward Joseph, is not now so characteristic, and the upturned hand and eyes of Joseph are omitted. The commissioner of the replica had evidently requested a certain amount of softening.

⁵⁵ Cf. Wolfgang Stechow, "Jacob Blessing the Sons of Joseph—From Early Christian Times to Rembrandt," in the *Gazette des Beaux Arts*, 6th series, vol. XXIII (1943), pp. 193 ff. The legend is recounted in *Pesikta Rabbathi*, ed. Friedmann, Vienna, 1880, pp. 11b–12b. Cf. also Louis Ginzberg, *The Legends of the Jews*, II, Philadelphia, 1910, p. 136.

⁵⁶ Frits Lugt rightly calls attention to the fact that the Bible narrative makes no reference to an angel, but to a man. It was in Christian art that the angel was first substituted. Compare his article "Man and Angel" in the *Gazette des Beaux Arts*, 6th series, vol. XXV (1944), pp. 265 ff.

⁵⁷ Cf. A. Heppner: "Moses zeigt die Gesetzestafeln," in the periodical *Oud Holland*, LII (1935), pp. 241 ff.

⁵⁸ The David in this painting brings Spinoza to mind, as had already been pointed out by André Charles Coppier, "Rembrandt et Spinoza," in *Revue des Deux Mondes*, XXXII (1916), pp. 160 ff. A similar Spinoza portrait is reproduced by Ernst Altkirch, *Spinoza im Portrait*, Jena, 1913, fig. 8. If it is taken for granted that the "Saul and David" had already been painted in the fifties, this assumption becomes more credible. At that time Spinoza (born 1632) was in his early twenties, and the David could also have been depicted at this age. It is of course also conceivable that Rembrandt may have made a drawing of a younger Spinoza, who had attracted general attention by his scholarship, and later utilized it in his painting.

182

BIBLIOGRAPHY

I. REMBRANDT—LIFE AND ART

A. General Works

OTTO BENESCH, Rembrandt: Werk und Forschung. Vienna, 1935.

——————, Rembrandt. New York, 1957.

WILHELM BODE, Die Meister der hollaendischen und flaemischen Malerschulen. Leipzig, 1921.

C. HOFSTEDE DE GROOT, Die Urkunden ueber Rembrandt. The Hague, 1906. (English edition in Bode-Hofstede de Groot, vol. VIII; see first item under B).

RICHARD HAMANN, Rembrandt. Berlin, 1948.

ARTHUR M. HIND, Rembrandt. Cambridge, Mass., 1932.

FRITS LUGT, Wandelingen met Rembrandt in en om Amsterdam, 1915; enlarged German edition: Mit Rembrandt in Amsterdam. Berlin, 1920.

CARL NEUMANN, Rembrandt, 4th edition. Munich, 1924.

JAKOB ROSENBERG, Rembrandt. Cambridge, Mass., 1948.

SEYMOUR SLIVE, Rembrandt and his Critics 1630–1730. The Hague, 1953.

WILHELM R. VALENTINER, Rembrandt und seine Umgebung. Strassburg, 1905.

——————, "Rembrandt at the Latin School," in his book *The Art of the Low Countries*. Garden City, N. Y., 1914.

WERNER WEISBACH, Rembrandt. Berlin, 1926.

B. Paintings

WILHELM BODE and C. HOFSTEDE DE GROOT, The Complete Work of Rembrandt: History, Description and Heliographic Reproductions of the Master's Pictures, with a Study of his Life and his Art. 8 volumes, Paris, 1897–1906.

C. HOFSTEDE DE GROOT, A Catalogue Raisonné of the Most Eminent Dutch Painters. VI. (Rembrandt and Maes). London, 1916.

The Paintings of Rembrandt, edited by ABRAHAM BREDIUS. Vienna and London, 1937.

Rembrandt: Selected Paintings. With an introduction and notes by TANCRED BORENIUS. London, 1942.

W. R. VALENTINER, Rembrandt: Des Meisters Gemaelde (Klassiker der Kunst), 3rd edition. Stuttgart and Berlin, 1909.

——————, Noch einmal "Die Judenbraut," in *Festschrift Kurt Bauch*, Berlin, 1957, pp. 227 ff.

——————, Rembrandt: Wiedergefundene Gemaelde (Klassiker der Kunst), 2nd edition. Berlin and Leipzig, 1923.

C. Etchings

George Bjoerklund with the assistance of Osbert H. Barnard, Rembrandt's Etchings True and False. Stockholm, London, New York, 1955.

The Complete Etchings of Rembrandt, edited, with an introduction, by CONSTANCE SCHILD. New York, 1937.

ARTHUR M. HIND, A Catalogue of Rembrandt's Etchings. Chronologically arranged and completely illustrated, 2nd edition. London, 1923.

LUDWIG MUENZ, A Critical Catalogue of Rembrandt's Etchings. London, 1952.

WOLDEMAR VON SEIDLITZ, Die Radierungen Rembrandts, 2nd edition. Leipzig, 1922.

HANS W. SINGER, Rembrandt: Des Meisters Radierungen, 2nd edition. Stuttgart and Leipzig, 1910.

D. Drawings

OTTO BENESCH, The Drawings of Rembrandt. First complete edition in 6 volumes, London, 1954–1957.

HOFSTEDE DE GROOT, Die Handzeichnungen Rembrandts, Versuch eines beschreibenden und kritischen Katalogs. Haarlem, 1906.

FRANZ LIPPMANN and C. HOFSTEDE DE GROOT, Original Drawings by Rembrandt van Rijn, reproduced in phototype. Leipzig, 1888; The Hague, 1911.

W. R. VALENTINER, Rembrandt: Des Meisters Handzeichnungen (Klassiker der Kunst). I, Stuttgart-Berlin-Leipzig, 1925; II, 1934.

II. THE JEWS IN AMSTERDAM

HERBERT I. BLOOM, The Economic Activities of the Jews of Amsterdam in the 17th and 18th Centuries. Williamsport, Penna., 1937.

H. BRUGMANS and A. FRANK, Geschiedenis der Joden in Nederland. Part I, Amsterdam, 1940.

JAKOB FREUDENTHAL, Spinoza: Leben und Lehre. 2nd edition, by Karl Gebhardt. Heidelberg, 1927.

CECIL ROTH, The Life of Menasseh ben Israel, Rabbi, Printer and Diplomat. Philadelphia, 1934.

Die Schriften des Uriel da Costa. Mit Einleitung, Uebertragung und Regesten, herausgegeben von Karl Gebhardt. Heidelberg, 1922.

DAVID MOZES SLUYS, De oudste synagogen der Hoogduitsch-Joodsche gemeente te Amsterdam, 1635–1671. Amsterdam, 1921.

JACOB SAMUEL DA SILVA ROSA, Geschiedenis der Portugeesche Joden te Amsterdam, 1593–1925. Amsterdam, 1925.

JACOB ZWARTS, De eerste rabbijnen en synagogen van Amsterdam, naar archivalische bronnen. Amsterdam, 1929.

III. REMBRANDT AND THE JEWS

"Rembrandt als Joodsch Schilder, Rembrandt's kennis van het Hebreeuwsch," (Anonymous), De Vrijdagavond, II, 1, 1925, pp. 38 ff. and 61 ff.

ISRAEL ABRAHAMS, "Menasseh and Rembrandt," in By-Paths in Hebraic Bookland, Philadelphia, 1920, pp. 147 ff.

JULIUS BAB, Rembrandt und Spinoza. Ein Doppelbildnis im deutsch-juedischen Raum. Berlin, 1934.

184

BIBLIOGRAPHY

OTTO BENESCH, Artistic and Intellectual Trends from Rubens to Daumier. Cambridge, Mass., 1943, pp. 23 ff. (deals with one of Rembrandt's etchings for the *Piedra Gloriosa*).

ANDRÉ CHARLES COPPIER, "Rembrandt et Spinoza," in *Revue des Deux Mondes,* XXXI, 1916, pp. 160 ff.

JOHS. DYSERINCK, "Eene Hebreeuwsche inscriptie op eeneschilderij van Rembrandt," in *De Nederlandsche Spectator,* 1904, pp. 130 ff. and 315 ff.

KARL GEBHARDT, "Rembrandt und Spinoza," in *Chronicon Spinozanum,* IV, 1924–1926, pp. 160 ff.

——————, "Rembrandt und Spinoza. Stilgeschichtliche Betrachtungen zum Barock-Problem," in *Kant-Studien, Spinoza-Festheft,* Berlin, 1927, pp. 161 ff.

J. GOEKOOP-DE JONGH, "De man met het vergrootglas door Rembrandt," in *Bredius-Festbundel,* Amsterdam, 1915, pp. 53 ff.

HOFSTEDE DE GROOT, "Kende Rembrandt Hebreeuwsch?" in *Oud Holland,* XIX, 1901, pp. 89 ff.

MAX GRUNWALD, "Rembrandt's Neighbors," in *The Jewish Chronicle,* July 13, 1906, p. 38.

FRANZ LANDSBERGER, "Rembrandt's Synagogue," in *Historia Judaica,* VI, 1944, pp. 69 ff.

FRITS LUGT, "Rembrandt's Man with the Magnifying Glass: a New Identification," in *Art in America,* XXX, 1942, pp. 174 ff.

MANASSEH BEN ISRAEL, אבן יקרה: Piedra gloriosa; o, De la estatua de Nebuchadnesar. Amsterdam, 5415 (1655).

LUDWIG MUENZ, "Rembrandt's Synagogue and Some Problems of Nomenclature," in *Journal of the Warburg Institute,* III, 1939–40, pp. 119 ff.

J. S. DA SILVA ROSA, "Heeft Rembrandt het portrat van Chagam Saul Levi Morteyra geschilderd?" in *De Vrijdagavond,* III, 1, 1926, pp. 22 f.

ISRAEL SOLOMONS, "The Second Series of Illustrations for the Piedra Gloriosa of Manasseh ben Israel," in *The Jewish Chronicle,* July 27, 1906, pp. 31 ff.

CHARLES DE TOLNAY, "Intreprétation de la 'Fiancée Juive,'" in *L'Amour de l'Art,* XVI, 1935, pp. 277 ff.

A. M. VAZ DIAS, "Wie waren Rembrandt's Joodsche buren," in *De Vrijdagavond,* VII, 2, 1930, p. 22.

——————, "Rembrandt en zijn Portugeesch-Joodsche buurtgenooten," in *De Vrijdagavond,* VIII, 2, 1931, p. 121.

——————, "Rembrandt in conflict met zijn buursman Daniel Pinto," in *Oud Holland,* LIII, 1936, pp. 33 ff.

W. R. VALENTINER, Rembrandt and Spinoza. London, 1957.

H. VAN DE WAAL, Rembrandts Radierungen zur Piedra Gloriosa des Manasseh ben Israel, in the periodical *Imprimatur,* ein Jahrbuch fuer Buecherfreunde, vol. XII, 1954–1955, pp. 52 ff.

ALFRED WERNER, The "Jew" Rembrandt, in the periodical *Judaism,* VI, 1957, pp. 248 ff.

JACOB ZWARTS, "Rembrandt's Phoenix en het oude wapen der Portugeesch-Joodsche gemeente van Amsterdam," in *Oud Holland,* XLIII, 1926, pp. 61 ff.

——————, "Haham Saul Levy Morteyra en zijn portret door Rembrandt," in *Oud Holland*, XLIII, 1926, pp. 1 ff.

——————, The Significance of Rembrandt's "The Jewish Bride." Amersfoort, 1929.

IV. REMBRANDT AND THE BIBLE

BIALOSTOCKI, "Ikonographische Forschungen zu Rembrandts Werk," in *Muenchner Jahrbuch der Bildenden Kunst*, 1957, pp. 195 ff.

Rembrandt Bijbel, edited by C. HOFSTEDE DE GROOT. Part I (Old Testament), Amsterdam, 1906.

Rembrandt-Bibel mit Abbildungen, gewaehlt und eingeleitet von F. W. Bredt. Munich, 1927.

The Rembrandt Bible. A Selection from the Master's Graphic Work, by O. GOETZ. New York, 1941.

J. BRUYN, Rembrandt's keuze van bijbelse onderwerpen, Utrecht, 1959.

Das Buch Esther. Mit Bildern von Rembrandt. Berlin, 1923.

WILHELM BODE, "Pieter Lastman's Gemaelde der Susanna mit der Alten und seine Beziehungen zu den Darstellungen des gleichen Motivs von Rembrandt," in *Amtliche Berichte aus den Preussischen Kunstsammlungen*, XXX, 1908, pp. 57 ff.

JOHS. DYSERINCK, "Rembrandt's Hanna en Samuel in de Ermitage te St. Petersburg en de Bridgewater-Gallery te London," in *Leidsche Jaarboekje*, 1906, pp. 103 ff.

HERBERT VON EINEM, Der Segen Jakobs von Rembrandt, in *Bonner Beitraege zur Kunstgeschichte*, Bonn, 1949.

KURT FREISE, "Bathsebabilder von Rembrandt und Lastman," in *Monatshefte fuer Kunstwissenschaft*, II, 1909, pp. 202 ff.

R. GREEF, Rembrandt's Darstellungen der Tobiasheilung. Stuttgart, 1907.

RICHARD HAMANN, "Hagars Abschied bei Rembrandt und im Rembrandt-Kreise," in *Marburger Jahrbuch für Kunstwissenschaft*, VIII–IX, 1936, pp. 471 ff.

A. HEPPNER, "Moses zeigt die Gesetzestafeln," in *Oud Holland*, LII, 1935, pp. 241 ff.

CHARLES JOHN HOLMES, "Tobit and his Wife by Rembrandt and Dou," in *The Burlington Magazine*, IL, 1926, pp. 55 ff.

H. KAUFFMANN, "Rembrandt's Berliner Susanna," in *Jahrbuch der Preussischen Kunstsammlungen*, XLV, 1924, pp. 72 ff.

FRITZ SAXL, Rembrandt's Sacrifice of Manoah, London, 1939.

HUGO SCHMERBER, "Rembrandt's Simsonhochzeit," in *Kunstchronik*, Neue Folge, XVI, 1905, col. 97 ff.

WOLFGANG STECHOW, "Jacob Blessing the Sons of Joseph, from Early Christian Times to Rembrandt," in *Gazette des Beaux Arts*, 6th Series, XXIII, 1943, pp. 193 ff.

W. R. VALENTINER, "Rembrandt's Blinding of Samson" and "Rembrandt's Representation of Susanna," in *The Art of the Low Countries*. Garden City, N. Y., 1914, pp. 151 ff., and 164 ff.

186

——————, "Ein Altersentwurf Rembrandt's," in *Genius,* I, 1920, pp. 44 ff. (deals with the drawing "Nathan Reprimanding David").

LÉON WENCELIUS, Calvin et Rembrandt, Paris, 1937.

FRANZ WICKHOFF, Einige Zeichnungen Rembrandt's mit biblischen Vorwuerfen. Innsbruck, 1906.

RUDOLPH WUSTMAN, "Die Josephsgeschichte bei Vondel und Rembrandt," in *Kunstchronik,* Neue Folge, XVIII, 1907, pp. 81 ff.

——————, "Rembrandt und die Buehne," in *Galerien Europas,* I, Leipzig, 1905–1907, pp. 57 ff.

INDEX